This Just
Speaks to Me

This Just Speaks to Me

Words to Live By Every Day

HODA KOTB

WITH JANE LORENZINI

G. P. PUTNAM'S SONS

New York

PUTNAM
— EST. 1838 —

G. P. PUTNAM'S SONS
Publishers Since 1838
An imprint of Penguin Random House LLC
penguinrandomhouse.com

ISBN: 9780593191088
Ebook ISBN: 9780593191071

Printed in the United States of America
1   3   5   7   9   10   8   6   4   2

BOOK DESIGN BY KATY RIEGEL

Dedicated to endless hope

and healing in the name

of our next generation

Introduction

....

The truth is, I feel the same way about good quotes as I do about French fries—I'll never get tired of them! How about you? Honestly, I think most of us feel an endless need for a quick hit of inspiration. Like a galaxy of swirling stars, quotes draw us in with their mesmerizing beauty, each unique and compelling in its simplicity. We read a quote and then we read it again, soaking up a truth expressed by someone who—unlike us—was able to artfully transform a state of being into a series of well-crafted lines. *I'm crushed, I'm lonely, I'm elated, I'm grateful.* Thank goodness for these wordsmiths across the decades! Whether they were written using a quill pen or computer keys, we rely on powerful passages to quiet our fears or lift our spirits.

That's why, in 2019, we decided to gather a year's worth of my favorite quotes and publish them in *I Really Needed This Today.* The concept of tucking a variety of quotes into the pages of a book just made so much sense—a convenient, cozy place to turn to for encouragement as you started or ended your day. I thought it was so cool that every morning, people showed up at Rockefeller Plaza holding their copies. Someone would open the book to a calendar date or to a quote that was meaningful to them and ask me to sign on those special few inches. "This is *my* quote," they'd say, claiming ownership of the words that had soothed or fueled them. One reader shared that she used sticky notes to mark particularly notable quotes for her daughter, and she even penned mom insights on those pages, too. Isn't that lovely? Maybe one of those entries served as an unexpected conversation starter between the two. Another woman said she posts a daily quote from the book to her favorite group of women, explaining that "it's a way to at least say hello every day."

I've also been so gratified (but not surprised) to hear how many of you, thinking of others, offered the book to friends or family who were struggling and needed a boost. Countless numbers of people showed up at book signings with four, six, even eight books for me to sign as gifts for others. To me that means that we often don't know what to say to someone who's hurting; we can't find the right words. Sharing a book like this is a gesture we can make in hopes that somewhere in the 365 pages, there's a line or a story that will serve as a salve, or at least provide a moment of comfort. Quotes kindly rescue us and the people we love.

And, boy, did the world need rescuing in 2020, when the coronavirus swept across the globe, disruptive and deadly. Life for every person on the planet changed, testing our resolve, devastating our workforce, taking our loved ones. In New York City, empty streets were unnerving, makeshift morgues horrifying. Starving the virus completely reshaped the Big Apple and *every* community, leaving us all hungry for our "old" lives. In the heat of battle, health care warriors, first responders, truckers, grocery store workers, mail carriers, and so many others risked their lives for the greater good. Endless thanks. For me professionally, everything was odd, but at least I had a job. So many did not and were suffering. Working alone in Studio 1A was surreal, just me and one cameraman. I missed my colleagues and the buzz of a busy day. All of the energy in 30 Rock was drained and everything else was sanitized. We broadcast heartrending images from around the world day after day: trucks filled with coffins rolling into Italy, fragile seniors in wheelchairs being evacuated from their nursing homes. Thankfully, there were countless stories of unbridled kindness, too, some of which I'll share in this book, as a reminder that we helped one another during a very dark time. On the home front, like millions of families, Joel and I were laser-focused on keeping our two daughters healthy and happy. So many of us spent our days inside . . . worrying, washing hands, wondering. Everyone was on top of one another and on each other's last nerve from time to time. I was terrified for my mother, who handled the isolation with her signature strength and sunny outlook. Every Thursday, Joel, the girls, and I shared a meal with her via Zoom, an iPad "seated" at our respective dinner tables. "Oh, I'd love to taste your salmon!" she'd say, dressed for the special occasion, complete with full makeup. We all looked forward to our weekly dinner dates, grateful to technology for shrinking the miles between us.

Eventually, as each state began to reopen, our country was further rocked by the tragic death of George Floyd in Minneapolis. Across the nation, formerly empty streets filled with protesters expressing pain, anger, and demands for change. When violence unfolded and destruction devastated already struggling neighborhoods, our hearts broke yet again. Still, the urgency to do better, to treat one another equally, was potent, stronger than the growing pains that accompany real change. Has there been an awakening? Can we become a more color-blind society? I have faith, more than ever before, that we are trying. The year 2020 has been one of relentless challenge—physically, emotionally, mentally. I hope at the moment you're reading this that both our bodies and our communities are continuing to mend in an enduring way.

I suppose the unsettling truth about living is that the journey is a roller coaster of contentment and adversity. Life will never just become predictably smooth for any of us. From one day to the next, everything can change—and has—which must be why we crave quotes . . . brief, gentle reminders like "we We are blessed" or "It's not too late" or "Always be kind." I've realized, too, that a quote that may not resonate with you one day can suddenly become your quote because life has changed you. Words were just words until a deep pain or an immeasurable love ignited their power. *Now you're speaking my language!* And just like that, your heart is gently buoyed or happily bursting at the seams.

This Just Speaks to Me is simply another opportunity to celebrate our most beloved quotes, and to perhaps heal a bit. So, let's raise our mug of coffee or glass of wine and begin to keep the daily grind at bay for a moment or two. You can be sure that throughout the year ahead, as your perspective on life and your state of being inevitably change, *your* quotes await . . . to serve you and soothe you.

Ready? Let's do this.

> Get back up. Begin again. —*Brené Brown*

I'm a huge fan of watching graduation speeches, and Brené Brown crushed hers to the class of 2020 at her alma mater, the University of Texas at Austin. As we begin a new year, I'll let her words give us the boost we need to face whatever comes our way in the days ahead:

> To get back up from a fall, to get back up from a setback, to get back up from what we're in right now, you have to acknowledge you're down, that you've fallen, failed, made a mistake. You have to be brave enough to acknowledge that you're hurting, that you're sad, disappointed, grieving, feeling shame; whatever feeling you're in, you have to own it. We cannot begin again when we're dragging unspoken and unexplored emotions behind us. We have to be brave and curious and to dig into the feelings of a fall.

Brené goes on to say that her falls have taught her much more about who she is than any of her achievements have. Yes! Five powerful words: Get back up. Begin again.

> Don't take yourself seriously. We are here today, we are
> gone tomorrow, so enjoy every moment of your existence.
> —*Deepak Chopra*

I swear you contract peacefulness when you sit across from Deepak Chopra. His sense of calm is absolutely contagious. When I interviewed the *Metahuman* author, I asked him how he was doing. "I'm totally at peace," he replied. I believed him! When we began to talk about his favorite quote, Deepak offered his own words: "Don't take yourself seriously. We are here today, we are gone tomorrow, so enjoy every moment of your existence." He advised maintaining perspective on social media, saying that no matter what you say, there are people who will criticize, troll, and attack you. If you're taking yourself too seriously, you'll be offended for the rest of your life. "We become biological robots, constantly being triggered by people and circumstances into predictable outcomes, and that's a terrible way to live; you're at the mercy of every stranger on the street." Instead, Deepak suggests we focus our lives on embracing joy, maximizing the power of love, and finding purpose and meaning in our existence. See? *Ahhh.* Don't you just feel at peace right now?

A parent's day:
50% preparing to go somewhere
1% somewhere
49% preparing to leave somewhere

This is what it's like when our family decides to have a picnic in the park, a mere sixty yards from our house at the beach.

Step 1: Preparing for the picnic
Get the kids ready . . . find two matching shoes, and who has the sunscreen? "Honey, you *have* to have socks on." Then, "I'm hot!" Time to explain that a coat must be worn. Meantime, bag sandwiches, find mats to sit on, toys to entertain the kids, cram a wagon full of all the stuff.

Step 2: The picnic
No one's enjoying the picnic.

Step 3: Preparing to go home
Repack everything from step one while questioning why we ever went on a picnic.

> Motivation is what gets you started. Habit is what keeps
> you going.
> —*Jim Ryun*

I'm open to any ideas when it comes to breaking habits . . . snapping
a rubber band on my wrist, dumping detergent on discarded sweets
so I won't eat them, whatever. So, I was interested in what B. J. Fogg,
author of *Tiny Habits: The Small Changes That Change Everything*,
had to say. His approach was simple. "You take a routine you already
do, like putting on your pajamas, and you put the new habit right
afterward." B.J. then said to reinforce the habit with an affirmation,
like a fist pump along with the word "Awesome!" (He said emotions
cement habits.) When I asked B.J. to help me be more present, he
suggested that when I get home each day, I should put down my bag,
plug in my phone, and leave it there. Fist pump; awesome. I was willing to try, considering Haley had recently asked for my phone to
"check her emails." Ugh. Bottom line: I tried it, I liked it, I wouldn't
call it a habit just yet. Anything you'd like to change? Do it, then say
out loud: "Fist pump; awesome!"

Let me keep my distance, always, from those who think they have the answers. Let me keep company always with those who say "Look!" and laugh in astonishment, and bow their heads.

—*Mary Oliver*

We certainly were keeping our distance from one another amid the COVID-19 crisis. Very few airline flights were up and running, so I loved how one Southwest Airlines flight attendant kept her sense of humor during such a turbulent time. A video shows her addressing the *one* passenger on board:

Flight attendant: "Welcome aboard, Bob."
Bob: "Thank you."

Upon landing, she told Bob to call his grandmother and tell her it was his best flight ever.

When I saw you I fell in love, and you smiled because you
knew.
                                                    —*Arrigo Boito*

Hearts everywhere burst at the image of an eighty-eight-year-old
Massachusetts man in a bucket lift visiting his wife in a rehabilitation
center closed to family members during the COVID-19 pandemic.
Married for sixty-one years, Nick Avtges hadn't seen his beloved
Marion for a month, so with the help of a tree company, he found a
way up to her third floor. "They could have lifted me ten stories," he
said, "and it would not have bothered me." Wearing a mask and
gloves, Nick is seen standing in a white bucket outside Marion's window.
During their twenty-minute chat, Nick revealed a sign that
read "I Love You Sweetheart." His bride's response? "She said, 'I love
you too, more than you know.'" Used to seeing each other every day,
the two lovebirds were grateful to share time together. "He's been a
very devoted husband," said the facility president. "He never missed
a day." Oh my goodness. True love always finds a way!

You can call it the "Perfect Moment" when the universe aligns and the music in your head actually matches the music outside and all is well.   —*Hugh Elliot*

I still can't believe this happened. Waiting in a greenroom at *The Ellen DeGeneres Show*, I was driving Laura and Mary crazy playing the same song over and over. They are the loveliest women who work hair and makeup magic, and I was torturing them with the repeat button. I couldn't help it! The song "Underdog" by Alicia Keys is simply awesome. It's like an anthem for anyone who's scraped and clawed their way to victory, and you can't help but pump your fist when it's playing. Here's the magic moment: as I was cranking Alicia Keys's song, I turned around and ALICIA KEYS was walking past the dressing room! Whaaaaaaaaaaat????? I screamed her name and about passed out. How was this happening? She joined us and started singing along . . . with herself! I was hearing both the live and taped version of "Underdog"! Laura said, "I've worked at the *Today* show for twenty years. This is in my top five." Mine, too! Maybe a perfect moment is waiting for you today. Get ready!

> When you learn, teach. When you get, give.
>
> —*Maya Angelou*

I've never gotten choked up over a doughnut. Doughnuts make me happy! But I teared up when *Today* aired a story about an act of kindness that unfolded for an Ohio bakery owner. Emilie Smith owns the Tremont Goodie Shop, which her grandfather opened in 1955. When the COVID-19 crisis forced her to close her shop to foot traffic, Emilie cut back on staff and relied on to-go orders. Like so many businesses, the bakery was struggling and Emilie was terrified she'd lose the treasure that had been in her family for three generations. As Emilie was working on payroll one day, a longtime customer called in an order for his favorite doughnut: custard with chocolate frosting. The regular—who wanted to remain anonymous—offered to pay $1,000 for the sweet treat, the bulk of his stimulus check. "I couldn't talk, I was crying," Emilie said. She posted a photo of an older man's hand holding the packaged doughnut, a little red heart drawn on the bag. When you get, give. Even just a little.

> Blessed are the curious, for they shall have adventures.
>
> —*Lovelle Drachman*

At home, we have a whiteboard to write down for Haley what we've got planned for the day. I always include "go on an adventure," even if it's the simplest of tasks, like our walks to CVS. "Okay, Haley, the first stop on our adventure is going to a drugstore. Where is one?" She'll look around intently—"I know, I know!"—excited to be part of Team Adventure. "Haley," I'll say, "the next part of our adventure is finding a dog," and of course there are a million in New York walking around. "I see one!" she'll say, delighted. If we're stuck inside, I'll post a "Funny Walk Zone" in the hall. Now we can have a brief adventure acting silly, bopping across five feet of hallway. I still catch myself rushing her around to get things done, but I do make an effort to turn the mundane into a memorable moment as often as possible. A kid's imagination is bigger than any adventure we can take them on, so I do my best to spark Haley's and just let her roll.

> Everything worth doing starts with being scared.
>
> —*Art Garfunkel*

US astronaut Christina Koch spent 328 days on the International Space Station, setting a record as the first woman to spend nearly a year in orbit. The video of her we ran on *Today* showed her beaming face atop the space capsule after returning to Earth. Her joy was unbridled! She'd completed the mission, she'd realized her childhood dream of becoming an astronaut, and . . . she was home. "Within the first two minutes of being back on Earth I saw more people's faces than I'd seen in a year," she said. Welcome back, Christina! Her advice to us all: do what scares you and go after things that seem like they're out of reach.

(On a lighter note, Savannah Guthrie asked all of us on set what our first meal back from space would be.

Craig Melvin: Steak and my mom's mac n' cheese.

Al Roker: A big bowl of ice cream.

Savannah: Pizza.

Me: Fried chicken and mashed potatoes.)

What's broken can be mended. What hurts can be healed. And no matter how dark it gets, the sun is going to rise again.

I love the sun. My phone is filled with photos of the golden beauty rising, setting, and sparkling on turquoise ocean water. So, when I read about a song selected by a New York hospital to celebrate patients who'd recovered from COVID-19, I thought, *Perfect*. During the coronavirus crisis, weary hospital staff agreed that a feel-good song could lift everyone's spirits if it was blasted over the loudspeakers whenever a patient was taken off a ventilator or discharged. Someone with a very bright idea suggested the Beatles song "Here Comes the Sun." From that day forward, whenever a patient was extubated or released, a nurse would call the operator and say, "Code Sun." The uplifting music would then waft through the hospital, alerting both patients and staff of a win. The hospital reported twelve "Code Suns" in one day, which warmed hearts and provided a much-needed ray of hope.

Be the best version of yourself.

—Nellie Biles

As we try to stick to our New Year's resolutions, this quote may serve as a motivator. Olympic superstar Simone Biles shared with me on *Today* that her mother, Nellie, raised her to "be the best Simone" she could be—the best version of herself. "I tried to be other people because I looked up to them," Simone explained, "but as I got older I thought, *If I can be the best version of myself, then everybody gets that version, so we all win in the end.*" If you've wondered what must be going through Simone's mind before she competes, it's this very advice from her mom! Hmm . . . if that phrase can help Simone nail a double backflip with three twists, surely we, too, can be the best versions of ourselves today.

> Every time a child is born, the world is renewed in innocence.
>
> —*Boyd K. Packer*

One of the best things about children is how simply they see the world and everyone in theirs. Country music superstar Carrie Underwood got a glimpse of how her four-year-old son sees her when he came home from preschool one day. On Instagram, she posted little Isaiah's worksheet titled "All About My Mom." He was asked to fill in the blanks for various questions about Carrie: I think my mom is <u>70 years old</u>. My mom's job is <u>wash the laundry</u>. My mom is really good at <u>folding laundry</u>.

Hilarious! I love this because while we all know Carrie as a global celebrity, her little boy just sees and loves her as Mom. Pure, sweet love. (Hey, Carrie—since you're so good at folding laundry, c'mon over sometime!)

> Unexpected kindness is the most powerful, least costly, and most underrated agent of human change.
>
> —*Bob Kerrey*

Sure, social media has its negatives, but there are also so many beautiful stories about how it can be used to solve problems. During the coronavirus pandemic, a scared doctor's wife posted a request on Facebook, which led to an amazing solution for more than just her family. Emily Phillips was concerned about the potential deadly consequences of living with her physician husband as he treated COVID-19 patients. Their newborn, and she and her eight-year-old son, both asthma sufferers, were at great risk. When Emily's mother suggested she search for a mobile home to park in the driveway, she reached out on Facebook. Not only was Emily offered an RV, a group was formed online called RVs 4 MDs. Across the nation, spare mobile homes were matched with health care workers who needed to live separately from their loved ones. The images on Facebook were beautiful—grateful doctors, nurses, and paramedics holding thank-you signs and posting videos sharing their immense gratitude. What a clever and caring solution. That's how Americans roll!

> Sharing a bit of yourself, opening a window into your own world, is a good place to begin.   —*Jeff Greenwald*

I wasn't surprised by the emojis people chose to share most often during the pandemic. They truly reflected the wild swing of emotions we all were experiencing. An organization called Emojipedia tracked the most popular emojis selected during April 2020. Here are the top five:

1. Face with tears of joy
2. Loudly crying face
3. Pleading face with anxiety eyes
4. Rolling on the floor laughing
5. Red heart

The emojis I used most often were: face with medical mask, heart eyes, and red heart.

> Dedication, determination, and hard work will feed life
> into your dreams. —*LaDonna M. Cook*

Jenna turned me on to the Netflix documentary series *Cheer*, a show that changed the way many people think about cheerleading. The program followed the cheerleading team at Navarro College in Texas as the athletes prepared to compete in the national championships. Like a complicated cheerleading move, the show is a compelling combination of athletics, struggle, pain, love, and dedication. I got sucked in from the start, wowed by the kids' extraordinary strength and coordination, and by the no-nonsense but loving leadership of their coach, Monica Aldama. When Monica and cheerleaders Jerry Harris, Gabi Butler, and La'Darius Marshall were guests on our show, we loved surprising them with a visit from Houston Texans star J. J. Watt. He's a huge fan of *Cheer*, too! Monica and the kids seemed truly blown away by the popularity of the series, but now that we've had a peek into their sport and their lives, we can't imagine wanting to root for a team any more than we do for them. Mat talk: let's goooo, Navarro!

> Keep life simple.

COVID-19 forced us all to make life simpler in many respects. Countless ideas appeared on social media for easy ways to add a pop of fun to the day. When I saw someone's instructions for an easy "ice cream shop," I asked Joel to remove the screen in the window that leads out to our porch. Voilà! Now we could help Haley scoop ice cream and teach her a bit about exchanging money for a service. We brought a dime and an empty cake cone to the shop window and helped Haley fill the cone with vanilla ice cream, then top it with tons of rainbow sprinkles. Sure, the "staff" ate most of the profits, but we had a blast, all thanks to a simple idea and my favorite handyman.

In a gentle way, you can shake the world.

—*Mahatma Gandhi*

I met a pint-sized powerhouse just after Martin Luther King Jr. Day in 2020. Ten-year-old Gregory Payton was joined on set by his speech teacher, Zerita Sharp. Gregory was one of the children featured in the HBO documentary *We Are the Dream*, which highlighted an annual public speaking competition in Oakland, California. Young performers attend to present poems and speeches inspired by Martin Luther King Jr. As we all watched a video clip of Gregory speaking at the event, his small frame onstage was completely contradictory to his commanding oratory skills. When he finished, the crowd erupted! Back on set, Gregory's teacher had tears streaming down her face. "It's not a performance," Zerita said. "Each time is a blessing to hear." When Jenna asked the young man what he wanted to be when he grew up, Gregory beamed. "I want to be a preacher like Dr. King and my paw-paw." We were *not* surprised Gregory's grandfather was a preacher. Gregory, you have the gift of inspiration in your genes!

You have power over your mind,
not outside events. Realize this,
and you will find strength.

—MARCUS AURELIUS

Gosh, the mind. It can be so sneaky in what it chats about up there in our noggins, right? We have to show it who's boss and take control of the talking points: love, kindness, peace, joy, gratitude.

> And now that you don't have to be perfect, you can be good.
>
> —*John Steinbeck*

I love how open and honest—and hilarious—Amy Schumer is about life's imperfections. When her son was nearly one year old, she shared on social media that a name change was in order.

"It's now Gene David Fischer," she said, referring to her son's new name. "It *was* Gene Attell Fischer but we realized that we, by accident, named our son 'genital.'"

Ha! Both names are a tribute to comedian Dave Attell, a close friend of Amy and her husband.

Remember your why.

This quote could have hung on the wall of countless beleaguered businesses devastated by the economic shutdown during the pandemic. We send our love and support to every business owner struggling to reconnect with the spark of their original dream.

Bliss only finds those with open arms.

Tony Dungy and his wife, Lauren, have opened their arms and hearts to ten children. As advocates for foster care and adoption, the couple coauthored a children's book titled *We Chose You: A Book About Adoption, Family, and Forever Love.* On *Today*, Lauren explained that the main character, Calvin, works with his parents on a school project outlining his adoption journey. "He was planned, he was prayed for, and it's reassuring for him to know that." I love how the book not only gives parents ideas on how to approach a conversation with young kids, it also comforts the little ones. "We hope that it speaks to the kids and says, 'Hey, there's nothing weird, there's nothing bad about being adopted,'" Tony said. "'God just brought you in a different way to your family.'" The Dungys want the book to also serve as a reminder of how many kids are out there . . . waiting to be welcomed with open arms.

Challenges are what make life interesting and overcoming them is what makes life meaningful.

—*Joshua J. Marine*

Five weeks after Dylan Dreyer's baby, Oliver, was born, I packed up Haley for a weekend road trip and we headed to Dylan's house. Calvin, Dylan's older son, joined us as we loved on little Ollie. I asked Dylan how she was doing, and like all moms, she said she was in heaven but exhausted. Adding another child to the mix had her juggling breastfeeding, caring for Calvin, and missing naps. When our three-year-olds started banging on a miniature piano and drum set, I asked, "Is this okay, Dylan?" as I cradled sweet Ollie. She said, "It's great!" Boy, Dylan really was amazing, her joy overriding the chaos of a growing family. I'm so glad we got to spend a Sunday with Dylan and her kids, especially with the newest family member of all.

Excuses are for losers. —*Candace Cameron Bure*

As we try to stick to our New Year's resolutions, I think this quote from actress Candace Cameron Bure is some good, tough love. When I interviewed her for my "Quoted By" segment, she admitted that while the quote isn't very "warm and fuzzy," it's a tool she and her husband have used as parents. "This has been our family motto," she said. "My husband's been saying this since I've known him, so for twenty-five years. I think probably a coach had told him, or his dad." With two teenagers and a twenty-year-old, Candace explained why the quote is effective as a motivator. "I love this because it's not about being the winner, it's a character builder. It's saying there are no excuses. Just try. Go for it." Well, okay, then! Today, armed with our resolutions, let's imagine Candace shaking her head at us: "Nope . . . excuses are for losers."

One day you will wake up and all of a sudden the weight of the last few weeks, months, or even years will be lifted off your shoulders. You can't control when that day comes, all you can do is stay strong and trust that it is coming.

This is great news! Hold on.

HK

Grief is not a sign of weakness, nor a lack of faith. It is the price of love.

I was getting my nails done when I saw terrible breaking news scrolling across the salon's television screen. NBA superstar Kobe Bryant was dead. I couldn't process the concept for several seconds. Was it *the* Kobe? On this day in 2020, the world was in collective shock at reports that the forty-one-year-old and nine other people aboard a helicopter were killed when it crashed into a hillside on an extremely foggy morning in Calabasas, California. I remember feeling so crushed by the loss of everyone aboard, but when it was revealed that Kobe's nine-year-old daughter, Gigi, had died, it was like a wrecking ball to the heart. Several days after the crash, Haley and I were saying prayers before bedtime, and I told her we needed to add Vanessa (Kobe's wife) to our list, that she was someone who needed comfort. A few nights later, Haley pointed out that we'd forgotten to pray for Vanessa . . . and so we did. Peace to you, Kobe and Gigi, and we send our love to you, Vanessa, Natalia, Bianka, and Capri.

> Having somewhere to go is home. Having someone to love is family. Having both is a blessing.

Joel and I, like all parents, took every precaution we could to keep our daughters safe during the pandemic. I can't imagine how scary it was for families that included one or several members who worked in high-risk jobs. *Today* spoke with an emergency room doctor who moved into the backyard tree house to keep his wife and two young sons safe. "The biggest part of my decision to move out there was I could see in my wife's eyes that she was scared," said Jason Barnes. "I had to do something." The Barneses had previously equipped the tree house with electricity and a bunk bed but no running water. Jason's wife dropped off meals for him, which he often ate on the tree house porch so he could safely visit with his six- and nine-year-old. Imagine those boys watching their dad using a climbing wall or trapdoor to get into that tree house. Dad must have gotten tons of "cool" points! To all families who went above and beyond to stay safe during such unsettling times—thank you.

You come home,
make some tea,
sit down in your armchair,
and all around there's silence.
Everyone decides for themselves
whether that's loneliness or freedom.

Now that we've spent months together in quarantine during the pandemic, I have a feeling most of us will never take "freedom" for granted.

HK

> You don't choose your family. They are God's gift to you,
> as you are to them. —*Desmond Tutu*

Family truly is a gift. *Today* aired the story of a Samford University football player who surprised his stepdad one afternoon. Michael Musto and George Grimwade have been family since George was in second grade. In a video clip, you saw photos of young George wrapped around his stepdad's neck and Michael tying his stepson's tie as a teenager. Incredibly dear. As a surprise, George legally changed his last name to "Grimwade-Musto" and had "Musto" stitched on the back of his football jersey! Before a big game, the twenty-two-year-old shared the news with Michael, who was sitting in the stands. "You know how much I love you, right? And how I always treasure the time I have with you. How you're my world." He then showed Michael the paperwork. "I got my last name changed." Next, he turned to reveal the Musto jersey. Their embrace was epic as tears flowed between them. Michael choked out, "You're my son." Now the Musto name lives on in George.

January 30

> You're meant to be here. This moment is yours.
>
> —*Herb Brooks*

During one of our *Hoda & Jenna* shows featuring a live audience, we aired a video clip of a woman in a London subway who, when randomly asked to sing a song, absolutely crushed it. We decided to ask if anyone in the crowd had a hidden talent. Spotting a woman pointing at her friend, we encouraged her to stand up. What happened next gave everyone goose bumps. Chantel from Long Island proceeded to belt out the Whitney Houston song "I Wanna Dance with Somebody." Suddenly, we were at a live concert with a superstar! Her voice brought down the house, everyone clapping in rhythm to the song. In that one moment, we got to watch as a stranger unwrapped her gift right before our very eyes and ears.

> A book is a dream that you hold in your hands.
>
> —*Neil Gaiman*

On this day in 2020, we lost the Queen of Suspense. Author Mary Higgins Clark died at age ninety-two, several months after releasing her latest novel. With countless bestselling books, Mary wrote more than fifty novels that readers devoured, loving the engaging stories about women who had to find their way out of an unexpected dilemma. Kathie Lee and I interviewed her several times, and she was always dressed to the nines with coiffed hair, unique jewelry, and genuine warmth toward everyone. I'll never forget how dear she was to my mother, who's a huge fan, when we saw her in Florida. We were walking through a hotel lobby, and there she was! "Is that Mary Higgins Clark?" my mom gasped. When we approached her, Mary was so nice and even took a photo with her superfan. My mom's smile was huge! What a great memory for us both. MHC, your books will comfort us as we are reminded of your genius and grace, page by page.

Those who are busy planting love don't have time to throw stones.
                                                            —*Saint Dulce*

Wouldn't it be great if this appeared as everyone's screen saver on their computer and phone?

Disconnect with technology and reconnect with each other.

This is called a "digital detox," and it's often easier said than done. When a study came out linking cell phone use to kids' feeling stressed and even suicidal, we talked about it on the set of *Today*. Al Roker said he locks up his seventeen-year-old son's phone in a small safe at night. While Nick might not love the idea, our parenting and youth development expert did. "It's really healthy for kids to have a break from the potential twenty-four/seven of social interactions," Dr. Deborah Gilboa explained. "They also need good sleep, and it's really hard to ignore notifications." She did recommend giving the phone back to teens one or two years before they leave home so they develop their own methods of limiting their screen time before bedtime. Even my very young kids are drawn to phones and screens. I'm not close to needing a safe, but I love Al's idea. I'm all for anything that gives our kids a mental health break. (And grown-ups need a break, too!)

It's not the weight you carry,
but how you carry it.

—MARY OLIVER

The best of us do this with grit and grace, and even without anyone's noticing.

HK

> We must take care of our families wherever we find them.
> —*Elizabeth Gilbert*

My sometime cohost Andy Cohen posted a sweet photo of himself with his son when Benjamin turned one on this day in 2020. I love watching Andy's heart bloom through his parenthood journey as mine has raising my two daughters. When Carson showcased the father-son photo on *Today*, we couldn't help but give a shout-out to the surrogate who gave birth to baby Ben. Andy has long been advocating for changes to state and national gestational surrogacy laws, offering more flexibility and options to those who wish to grow their family via a third-party surrogate. "No one should have to forfeit the joy of raising a child—not in an era when modern medicine is performing new miracles every day," Andy said, "and when we have reached a wide consensus that the only prerequisite to forming a family is love." Enjoy this special day, Andy, and happy birthday, Ben!

> Those who bring sunshine to the lives of others cannot keep it from themselves.
> —*J. M. Barrie*

Every year, today is designated National Weatherperson's Day. In 2020, Al marked his forty-second year on the air, twenty-four of them on *Today*. On set, we gave him a cupcake and brief video walk down memory lane. When Al isn't on the show, it doesn't work as well. I remember a time when he was off for three days and everything seemed clunky. We practically mobbed him when he returned, happy to have the secret sauce back in the bottle. Something you should know, too—at the start of every long commercial break, Al grabs his coat. "I'm headed outside to say hi to everybody." The best.

The purpose of life is not
to be happy—but to matter,
to be productive, to be useful,
to have it make some difference
that you lived at all.

—LEO ROSTEN

I like how this quote changes the equation.

INSTEAD OF:

Life = Happiness

SOMETHING MORE LIKE THIS:

Usefulness + Honor + Compassion = Life

> To love a person is to see all of their magic and to remind them of it when they have forgotten.

Country star Jennifer Nettles of the group Sugarland gave radio stations a little tough love to remind them of whom they'd "forgotten." At the 2019 CMA Awards, Jennifer hit the red carpet wearing a white suit and a red cape with a message.

Written on the front: *Play Our F*@#n Records, Please & Thank You!*

Written on the back: *Equal Play*

Jennifer's goal was to alert viewers to unequal airplay and to urge country stations to stop overlooking female voices, a problem she says has existed for a long time. "These artists, women artists don't get the support on radio, then they don't get the support on tour," she explained, "and it's a cycle, a really vicious cycle." Jennifer said fans who want to help should reach out to the program director at their favorite country station and ask them to play more songs by female artists. She also suggests they make female-dominant playlists on streaming services and buy tickets for shows that feature female artists. Well, now . . . for some reason I really feel like downloading a Sugarland song!

> Get out of your comfort zone. Wake up the sleeping giant in you.
>
> —*Chia Thye Poh*

Leading up to Valentine's Day, *Today* invited two women and a dating expert to pare down a small group of men through a variety of dates. Thirty-four-year-old Chloe and fifty-one-year-old Lisa were fun, and every guy was kind and positive. When the pool of men shrunk to three, Melissa Hobley, chief marketing officer at OkCupid, had a great idea: "adventure dates." So, Chloe took her trio of men to a rock-climbing gym, and Lisa, a competitive ballroom dancer, took her guys salsa dancing. I've got to hand it to the men! Each had a great attitude, sweating and stumbling and laughing as he operated outside of his comfort zone. The ladies chose the man who'd handled the date best. I think you can learn a lot about a person when they're in a fish-out-of-water situation. I've watched Joel beautifully manage adventures . . . everything from a new job to learning to play guitar. Why not try something new with someone you don't know well *or* with someone you love dearly? Buh-bye, comfort zone!

> A new baby is like the beginnings of all things—wonder,
> hope, a dream of possibilities.   —*Eda J. LeShan*

I took five months off for maternity leave when I adopted my daughter Hope, and they were the best five months of my life. I felt a bit bad about being away from work for so long, but during that tiny window, I got to witness everything, and for that I'm extremely grateful. We stayed at the beach during those bonding moments, our favorite place on earth. I wore out my journal trying to capture this second miracle in my life:

Hope Catherine Kotb, asleep upstairs, peaceful, happy, and calming. What a soothing child. She looks up at you as if to say, "Mom, don't worry. Everything will be okay." She cries a little when she's hungry, but that's it. I wonder if that will be her personality. She loves to be talked to. Her smile melts me. I can't believe God has blessed me in this way.

One year later and Hope's demeanor is exactly the same . . . wildly observant and content with all around her. What a gift she is, always smiling.

Everyone needs a friend who will call and say, "Get dressed, we're going on an adventure."

In spring 2020, that adventure was searching for toilet paper.

Forget about being impressive and commit to being real.

If anyone should have their own talk show, it's Kelly Clarkson. When *The Kelly Clarkson Show* hit the airwaves, I was so happy for her. Kelly is honest, genuine, hilarious, crazy talented, caring—I could go on and on. She's frequently cohosted with me on *Today*, so when she invited me to her show, I was excited. Sitting across from Kelly on live television is exactly like being with her off-air. It's comfortable and fun, and everybody in the studio and at home loves her. The girl is the real deal all the time! With glasses of wine and a great live audience, we cried about the beauty of motherhood, laughed about how Kelly thought Joel and I were already married, and joked about my odd habit of drunk-texting her. (She said the musical group Pentatonix does, too!) What a blast. I love you, Kelly, and keep up the great work making us all feel welcomed and like we've known you forever.

Life gets very quiet before all the doors open.
I'm learning that what can feel like
loneliness is actually grace.
Rest.
Find your strength.
It will change soon.

—J. LYNN

This quote is calming, isn't it? It reframes loneliness as a productive pause, a chance to become our best selves just in time for the big breakthrough.

She found peace right where she was.

And for me, during the COVID-19 quarantine, I found it in the bathroom with the door locked . . . a few moments of peace and quiet. Still do.

> As soon as I saw you, I knew a grand adventure was about to happen.
> —*from* Winnie-the-Pooh

Valentine's Day for me has been love on steroids since my daughter Haley came into my life in 2017. Her birthday falls on Valentine's Day, so Joel and I celebrate not only our love but how much we love our birthday girl. Haley actually has two birthdays—the day she was born, and the day she was born to us, February 14. My only wish each year has been for Father Time to please slow down so I can enjoy every precious ticktock with Haley, and now Hope, too. My daughters are my miracles, and Joel—among many other wonderful things—is the guy who turned Valentine's around for me. Not only did I meet my ex-husband on Valentine's Day, the paperwork for my divorce from him arrived on Valentine's Day, too. For years, I disliked the holiday, but now it's extra special. Needless to say, I'm the luckiest woman on this day and every day for the many ways I've been blessed. Sending love to you today!

Be good to as many people as possible.

Poet and artist Cleo Wade seems like she's wise beyond her thirty years. Her poems and writings, somehow, just have a way of soothing your soul. I loved a story Cleo shared about celebrating the one hundredth birthday of a friend's grandpa, whom she asked for advice about living a meaningful life. He fought in World War I, lived through the Depression and the civil rights movement, and twice saw Barack Obama become president. His answer to Cleo was, "Be good to as many people as possible." How beautifully simple. He said not only did the advice stick with him and serve him throughout his life, it also "got [him] to one hundred."

> Doing nothing for others is the undoing of ourselves.
>
> —*Horace Mann*

So true, and we often need a boost along the way. That's why country music superstar Brad Paisley and his wife, Kimberly, started the Store, a nonprofit facility that provides free groceries to people who've lost their job or are going through tough times. When I talked with Brad on *Today* about the project, he said they wanted the shopping experience to feel routine and dignified, including allowing customers to select their own food. When they opened the Store in March 2020, the organization never imagined how many additional people would soon need help. "We had about a week of operating like we expected when we opened in March, and here we are opening up something like this when, basically, all hell breaks loose," Brad said. "Now we're already serving three times the amount of people we expected right away." Great work, Brad and Kimberly! You're helping people heal so that one day they can overcome.

> Being brave isn't the absence of fear. Being brave is having that fear but finding a way through it. —*Bear Grylls*

I've scribbled in journals for many years and I still do. I'm so glad Jessica Simpson has since she was fifteen, because all the entries helped her compile her 2020 memoir, *Open Book*. I interviewed the singer and fashion mogul right before her book was released. Pardon the cliché, but Jessica strikes me as someone who's as beautiful on the inside as she is on the outside. She's honest, genuine, unabashedly vulnerable, and she exhibits the same qualities in her writing. "It's about walking through fear and it being okay to be afraid. And the other side of fear is what's so beautiful. That's when you get the reward." Jessica writes about being sexually abused as a child, using diet pills to manage her weight, marriage, living in the limelight, and her decision to quit drinking in 2017. Now healthy, happily married, and a mom to three children, Jessica is vibrant and grateful. "I want to show people the obstacles I've had to get through and the tools that I have now to go back and face them."

New energy is entering your life. Changes are happening for you. Things are getting better. Everything is aligning. Blessings are coming.

Yes! Put out the welcome mat . . . they're coming!

HK

One minute you're young and fun . . . the next minute you're turning down the radio in the car to see better.

Turns out lots of people do this when they parallel park! Ha!

> Now and then it's good to pause in our pursuit of happiness and just be happy. —*Guillaume Apollinaire*

Hope is at her happiest when our bedtime routine is under way. She loves every step! In the bathtub, she smiles and splashes as I scrub her down. "Baba?" My little girl is now ready for her bottle. Then she points to her stack of books. One of her favorites features dogs, which she asks for by saying, "Woof! Woof!" After we read, snuggled in our bed, I hold her in my arms and sing "Twinkle, Twinkle, Little Star" as I slowly sway her back and forth. As she drifts off, I lay her in her crib and give her a soft lovey blanket to nestle with as she falls asleep. (Mommy's not far behind.) Precious Hope, our nightly routine makes me so happy, too.

Sometimes when you're in a dark place you think you've been buried, but you've actually been planted. Be patient . . . your time to grow is coming!   —*Christine Caine*

Dark places are scary. I love how this quote shines a bright light in the corners, redefining the space. Maybe we're a spring crocus instead of a tree root.

You create your own calm.

I turned to throwback television during the pandemic to calm my nerves. Watching episodes of *Modern Family* and *Friends* was a convenient way to escape the endless news cycle, which had literally gone viral. Television programs and movies from "the old days" took me back to a time without so many worries. Did you feel that way? All of a sudden your heart rested for a while, right? If you need a moment of calm today, I highly recommend the movie *Maid in Manhattan*. *Sweet Home Alabama* works, too.

I get awkward when someone compliments me.
Someone: You look pretty.
Me: Happy birthday.

They say we get wiser as we get older, but I've found that there's so much to learn from people of all ages. A page at NBC named Bridget Yassme, who is in her twenties, taught me a wonderful phrase one day as I was complimenting her work ethic and all-around grounded nature. "You're humble and truly a bright light," I told her, and added a few more attributes I admire about her. When I was done, Bridget looked at me and said, "I received that." Wow. I let that sink in. "I love that," I replied. She told me that for a long time she never knew what to say when someone shared something nice about her to her face. (I'm the same way!) "One day I just thought how kind it would be for me just to receive it." I think Bridget is right. Her phrase is almost better than "thank you." It says, *What you've said to me is inside of me now. I'm not deflecting it, I'm receiving it. I accept your kind gift.*

> Few are those who see with their own eyes and feel with their own hearts. —*Albert Einstein*

I think in this day and age of likes and thumbs up and thumbs down, it's more difficult to be unaffected by what other people think of us. This is a good reminder to be our unique selves, to dream our dreams, and to stay focused on living *our* best life.

The simple act of caring is heroic. —*Edward Albert*

Al and Craig—both fathers—asked several black dads how they felt about their kids' interacting with law enforcement following the death of George Floyd. Seith Mann said of his child, "I know a lot of people do tell their children, 'Be polite, be respectful,' and I will certainly tell my son that. But I also recognize that that is not a guarantee of his safety." The agonizing Floyd video hit home for Morgan Scott Tucker. "There's probably not a black dad who hasn't imagined that being their son. I'd like to say that I was outraged and grief-stricken, but I think numb is probably what I really felt, because we've seen this before." When Ken Simril said black fathers must have uncomfortable conversations with their kids about being black in America, Craig and Al agreed. "My job as a father is to say, 'Yes, this is out there; you've got to be aware of it,'" Al said, "But you can't let it rule your life. And I've gotta help him find that balance."

> Nothing in the universe can stop you from letting go and
> starting over.
> —*Guy Finley*

My name will never be used in the same sentence as the word "fashionista." Heck, my mom chooses all of my work clothes. That's why I had a lot to learn from Lyn Slater when I met her on *Today*. At sixty-six, she has a life story as interesting as her message to women. During fashion week in New York City, the then–sixty-year-old was mistaken by photographers for a professional model as she waited for a girlfriend on the street. When her friend arrived, she laughed at the flashing cameras and said, "You're an accidental icon!" That term became the name of Lyn's blog and her Instagram account, and the road sign for her journey to being signed to multiple national campaigns. Now retired from teaching, Lyn hopes she inspires women of all ages. "You do not have to accept the box that society puts you in," she says. "Reinvent yourself the way you want to be." I love that, and I loved her advice for identifying your personal style: Choose three words that best describe you. Got 'em? Dress like that!

You are not lazy, unmotivated, or stuck.
After years of living your life in survival mode,
you are exhausted. There is a difference.

If this is you, may it be a point in time, and one that passes very soon.
Revival mode is close . . .

Whatever you must do today, do it with the confidence of a four-year-old in a Batman cape.

Speaking of superheroes, the families of health care workers during the COVID-19 crisis certainly behaved like them. A mom in Massachusetts was weary of reading comments online saying health care workers "knew the risks" when they went into health care and "signed up for" a career that included potentially infecting loved ones. So, Stephanie Scurlock posted a family photo on Instagram. In it, her three young children were dressed in their physician father's scrubs, the light-blue pants and shirts oversized. One daughter wore his stethoscope around her neck. The oldest daughter held a sign that read: "Not all heroes wear capes. Some wear scrubs . . . like our daddy. Stay home." Under the photo, Stephanie thanked anyone on the health care front lines and offered her prayers. She told *Today* that her family was doing everything they could to stay healthy while living with her husband, Joshua, a chief general surgeon. Precautions included Joshua's showering immediately upon coming home, separate laundry loads, and a constant whirlwind of disinfectant wipes. Thank you, Scurlocks, and all brave families living with heroes.

> The two things in life you are in total control over are your attitude and your effort. —*Billy Cox*

I think a big component of stress is feeling like life is out of control. *What's happening???* I like this quote because working hard with a smile on our face is something we *can* control. Yes, easier said than done, but possible.

> You're off to Great Places! Today is your day! Your mountain is waiting. So get on your way! —*Dr. Seuss*

Good ol' Dr. Seuss was born on this day. (Did you know his full name was Theodor Seuss Geisel? I didn't.) I love reading his books to my kids because we all just feel good after we're done. We're ready to go! There's something so uplifting about the way his simple words and clever drawings encourage us to be kind and curious. "Oh the thinks you can think up if you only try!" In all, Geisel wrote and illustrated more than forty children's books after nearly giving up on his dream of becoming a children's author. His first book was rejected by publishers twenty-seven times! A chance meeting with a friend who'd become a children's book editor became the break he needed. One last fun fact: Geisel added "Dr." to his pen name because his father had always wanted him to practice medicine. Happy birthday, Dr. Seuss!

A diamond is a chunk of coal that did well under pressure.

—HENRY KISSINGER

We do tend to sparkle after we've proven ourselves!

> When we share those stories we've been scared to share, voicelessness loses its wicked grasp. —*Jo Ann Fore*

Valerie Bertinelli. Don't you just smile when you think of her? Her fresh face and sparkling wit make her feel like an on-screen friend, and she's someone we've loved to watch in old sitcoms and now on the Food Network. But in 2020, Valerie opened up on *Today* about her decades-long, complicated relationship with food. "I've been losing the same ten pounds for the past fifty years," she said, shaking her head. "It can't be about the ten pounds anymore." As blessed as she knows she is, Valerie said her life has also included chapters of pain and sadness. While food has always soothed her, she said her new goal is to share her feelings out loud and to try to love herself as is. "I might not lose any weight on this journey, but I may just lose the weight that's sitting on my shoulders and on my heart," she said. We hear you, Valerie. We hear you finding your voice. (One month into her journey, Valerie said she was getting better at feeling things and moving on instead of suppressing her emotions.)

There is always hope.

When I feed my one-year-old daughter, Hope, each night, I'll ask, "Can I have a hug?" She looks right at me and then lays her head on my neck, nuzzling it. This beautiful child is like a ray of sunshine, warm and bright. I can easily make her laugh, which I adore. All I have to do is put up my pointer finger, and when she tries to touch it, I pull it away. She busts up like I'm Jerry Seinfeld! No one's funnier than me in that moment. Haley calls Hope her "little buddy kid" and wants her nearby. Boy, I'm lucky. Hope has blessed our family with her calm, sweet temperament. We love you, our little buddy kid.

> In the blink of an eye, something happens by chance—when you least expect it—sets you on a course that you never planned, into a future you never imagined.
>
> —*Nicholas Sparks*

I think we're all trying to blink away what unfolded in 2020, doing our best to reimagine our future. May today offer a dose of hope and joy . . . and perhaps a bit more clarity.

No one can close the door that God has opened for you.

When I sat down with singer-songwriter Ciara, every favorite quote of hers was better than the last! You see the one she chose above, but she also shared "Just put one foot in front of the other," moving her arms in slow motion, wearing a warrior face as she said it. "I always say to people, 'Just put one foot forward, even if your feet feel heavy and you feel like you're moving slow,'" she said. "You're making progress in that one little step." I've always loved Ciara's music, but now I'll listen with even more admiration for her and her faith in herself and God. "No matter what anyone says—it can be a hater, it can be an executive who tells you a song is not going to work— everyone can have opinions, but the reality is, no one can close the door that God has opened for you." So inspiring! I also love what Ciara suggested to do when life feels chaotic: "Be still." In other words, stop trying to control everything.

Here is the world. Beautiful and terrible things will happen. Don't be afraid. —*Frederick Buechner*

When *Today* broadcast live from Universal Orlando, I picked up the flu. Ugh. I wore a mask on the plane ride home and, upon landing, went directly to the doctor. Yep—I had the A strain of the flu. My biggest fear was infecting my girls, so I kept my distance as much as a mommy can. I bathed myself in Purell each time I saw the girls, who didn't understand why we had to be apart so much. Whenever Hope saw me, she crawled toward me like a thirsty desert dweller toward an oasis. Haley was frustrated but melted my heart when she said, "If I kiss you, it will make it better." Who needs Tamiflu when you have the sweetest little nurse? I was so happy when I finally recovered and was free to hug and kiss my little ones . . . and my big one, too.

> When we give cheerfully and accept gratefully, everyone is
> blessed. —*Maya Angelou*

When we were younger, my sister and brother and I thought gadgets were a great gift idea for my parents on special occasions—a very grown-up gesture. Whenever their birthdays or a holiday rolled around, we'd agree to pool our money to buy them a small appliance. "Let's get them a toaster!" Maybe it was because hand mixers and coffee grinders were relatively inexpensive, and they looked substantial wrapped up as a gift. You can bet that whenever my mom or dad felt in dire need of a crepe maker or a yogurt maker, one was at the ready in a cupboard. I realize now how kind it was of them to react with pure excitement and gratitude for yet *another* gift with a plug.

> Here's to strong women. May we know them. May we be them. May we raise them.

During Women's History Month, Savannah and I sat down with women involved in a club called Chief. In 2019, two female executives formed the organization to support women in their journey to land leadership roles in business. Cofounder Lindsay Kaplan said women who are alone at the professional table often look for another job. "If we can bring them together, they're more likely to stay and create a lasting change in their companies and beyond," she explained. One young club member shared a significant lesson she's learned on the job. "I had to get over not always being liked," she said. Sharon Leite, CEO of the Vitamin Shoppe, added that female fellowship is important because leading can be isolating, saying, "It's nice to have a place where you can have a conversation and you're not being judged." Founded in New York, Chief is now expanding nationally and is two thousand members strong. I'm certainly grateful for the women in my life who have lifted, and continue to lift, me up. And for the two little girls who do, too!

There is no such thing as a supermom. We just do the best
we can.   —*Sarah Michelle Gellar*

Mom or dad shaming. The worst.

> Helping others is the key duty for everyone on this earth who is remotely capable to do so. —*Joanna Krupa*

Helping is something we can teach our kids very early in life. When we interviewed child development expert Dr. Deborah Gilboa on *Today*, she said that getting kids involved with daily chores is good for them and helps produce "problem solvers of good character." When she outlined what chores are appropriate for what age group, I paid attention to my kids' grouping: eighteen months to three years, the "Me do it myself!" age, as Deborah put it. She cautioned not to give them a chore parents will end up redoing, because that would teach them their help isn't needed. "Let them do one part, like hold the dustpan while you sweep." Actually, Haley loves to help me with the laundry. When the dryer beeps, she yells, "Mommy, it's ready!" I hand her a piece of folded clothing and she puts it in the correct pile: Hope's pile, her pile, our pile. I never, *ever* considered that doing laundry could be fun, but with her by my side, it is.

> Music and rhythm find their way into the secret places of
> the soul. —*Plato*

Carson Daly and I share a passion for music, and we love to listen to each other's favorites. I'm not surprised that he was drawn to the story of Wintley Phipps, whom he interviewed about his foundation, the US Dream Academy. A minister and Grammy-nominated gospel singer, Wintley came up with the idea while singing for inmates. "So many of these young men looked like my sons," he said, "and a dream was born in my heart." The academy is a tutoring and mentoring program for kids whose parents are in jail. "You have to increase the density of caring, loving adults in the life orbit of kids," he explained, "when their parents become incarcerated." When you listen to Wintley talk or sing, you instantly sense his passion for whatever he's involved with. If you Google "'Amazing Grace' Wintley Phipps," you'll see him preaching and then belting out "Amazing Grace." Amazing! Way to shine light on the power of dreams and music, Carson. (And by the way, I've got about five new songs I want to play for you.)

> Could a greater miracle take place than for us to look through each other's eyes for an instant?
>
> —*Henry David Thoreau*

We did this more often during the pandemic. Neighbors met for the first time and many looked out for each other. I love what happened after British chef Anthony O'Shaughnessy posted this on Twitter: "I've been feeding the old man next door for about a month now. I ring him before dinner so I know to make extra." His followers began to tweet food photos and stories about how they, too, were cooking for neighbors. The plated food photos were amazing! Chef Anthony said that he and his neighbor are now friends. "I realized that my meals are giving him a great experience while he is at home," he said, "and it has encouraged me to make them as delicious as possible. . . . How much joy can I put into a plate of food?"

Whatever you are not changing, you are choosing. Read that again.

Okay, all right. You're saying that you don't want to hear any belly-aching if I'm not making an effort to pursue what *I say* I want.

Service to others is the rent you pay for your room here on earth. —*Muhammad Ali*

Thin Mints are my favorite Girl Scout cookies . . . an entire sleeve of them. I've devoured them for most of my life, and an incredible woman we featured on *Today* has been selling them since 1932! Ronnie Backenstoe joined the Scouts at ten years old, and now, at ninety-eight, she still wears her uniform and sets up a table at her retirement community in Wernersville, Pennsylvania. What a super Scout! In 2020, girls in Troop 1814 joined Ronnie to sell those beloved boxes. She told us, "I love to talk to the little girls today and tell them what I sold cookies for when I started—fifteen cents!" Ronnie said her late husband called her "the Peanut Butter Kid" because she loves Do-si-do sandwich cookies so much. Her love for the cookies and the organization spans eighty-eight years. "Girl Scouts is one of the best organizations in the world," Ronnie said. "It teaches children how to live life and how to treat other people and to do service for other people who need help." Love that. Keep rockin' it, Ronnie!

> I am a great believer in luck. The harder I work, the more
> of it I seem to have. —*Coleman Cox*

On St. Patrick's Day the year Carson Daly's fourth daughter was born, he came across what he felt was the perfect name. He'd just received the results of an Ancestry DNA kit confirming he was 98 percent Irish and was browsing through baby names connected with his heritage. "On St. Patrick's Day morning," he said, "I stumbled on Goldie." Goldie! So cute. Carson said that he and his wife, Siri, loved not only the name but also the fact that "Go Go" was their final child . . . a pot of gold at the end of their family rainbow. (Goldie's middle name, Patricia, honors Carson's beloved mom, who passed away in 2017.) I sure hope you have good fortune today, and don't forget to wear a wee bit o' green!

LAUNDRY

Washing: 45 minutes

Drying: 60 minutes

Putting away: 7–10 business days

*Small print: "putting away" may mean "piling in a corner."

> You are imperfect, permanently and inevitably flawed. And
> you are beautiful. —*Amy Bloom*

Just when I thought I couldn't love Olympic gymnast Simone Biles any more, I read a heartfelt piece she posted on Instagram. It began, "Let's talk about competition." But she wasn't referring to gymnastics. Instead, she wrote about how weary she is of the daily comments people make about her appearance. Using the hashtag #NOCOMPETITION, Simone wrote, "Today I say I am done competing VS. beauty standards and the toxic culture of trolling when others feel as though their expectations are not met . . . because nobody should tell you or I what beauty should or should not look like." While she said she's learned to ignore most of the negativity, Simone admitted some comments are hurtful. "I'd be lying if I told you that what people say about my arms, my legs, my body . . . how I look in a dress, leotard, bathing suit or even casual pants hasn't gotten me down at times." Of course! This seemingly superhuman athlete is human. You're beautiful, Simone, and so is your message. It's as powerful as you are.

And if you're ever feeling lonely, just look at the moon. Someone, somewhere, is looking right at it, too.

Sigh . . . a lunar link.

It is not how much we have, but how much we enjoy, that makes happiness. —*Charles Spurgeon*

This is my daughters having more fun playing with the gift wrap than the gift.

> The way we talk to our children becomes their inner voice.
>
> —*Peggy O'Mara*

When my *Today* colleague Dylan was sharing a story about her sweet son with Maria Shriver and me, she mentioned, "Calvin's shy." In a kind manner, Maria suggested Dylan consider *not* using adjectives like that. Dylan said, "But I'm shy, Calvin's shy . . ." Maria offered that when we label our kids, they grow into what we say they are instead of who they're meant to be. That really struck me. Many times I've seen kids lean into their parents when a stranger approaches. Heck, I've *caused* that behavior at book signings. Mom will wrap an arm around her daughter and say, "Oh, she's just shy." Her intention is good; those words are meant to comfort me or whomever the child eases away from. *It's not you. She does it with everyone.* But could the gesture be negative for the little one? Maybe. Dylan has mentioned Maria's thought to me several times, repeating, "I want Calvin to be Calvin." Both of us will now choose our words more wisely around our little sponges.

I finally realized that people are prisoners of their phones . . . that's why it's called a "cell" phone.

Yes! And an iPhone because "i" can't put it down! Let's try to "break out" for a good chunk of time today.

H.O.P.E.
Hold on, pain ends

When you're in the thick of it, pain feels like it's moved into your heart for good. *I'll never be the same.* When my father died suddenly when I was in college, my world went dark. How could I carry on with a boulder crushing my heart? But, as they say, time heals. My heart still aches to have my dad in my life—especially now that I have children—but life goes on, and we must treasure the precious time we have with the people we love.

> Your life requires your mindful presence in order to live
> it. Be here now. —*Akiroq Brost*

Anthony Tarantino has a mind full of opinions, and I love when he shares them from the floor of the NBC studios. A veteran cameraman, Anthony will often offer an opinion about something that's just aired. "Okay, that guy should have gone to prison," he'll say, his head sticking out from behind the camera. One day, we were all chatting about using our phones to tape our kids . . . walking, talking, losing baby teeth. Anthony chimed in. "Y'know what I did for all those years? I had a VHS camera and I was taping every single thing my kids did. I kind of missed all the moments. Now I've got forty VHS tapes in my basement and I've watched them . . . maybe twice." Gosh, nowadays a camera lens is simply an extension of our eyeballs! I'm certainly guilty, and honestly, I'll continue to capture moments on camera (especially because my memory is fading). Still, if I hear Anthony's voice in my head saying, *Um, you probably won't ever watch that video again*, I'll consider soaking up the moment . . . old-school style.

> Gratitude unlocks the fullness of life. It turns what we
> have into enough, and more. —*Melody Beattie*

I know everything felt off-kilter for all of us during the coronavirus crisis. Sweeping change was under way across our home and work lives. I decided to share my own odd reality at the *Today* show because I knew everyone was experiencing change in so many ways. I started recording on my phone as soon as I exited the car at four thirty in the morning. The plaza where NBC holds its packed concert series was empty. My "Good morning" to one or two people inside 30 Rock echoed off the walls. When I entered my dressing room, a "This area has been cleaned/disinfected" card lay on my desk. My beloved Mary and Laura—makeup and hair geniuses—were home, so I did my best. Our studio crew was down from fifteen to a single cameraman. How strange it was to be alone at the desk. Normally, there is so much organized chaos! I missed it all. On the other side of this, I'm sure we'll all be grateful for things we once took for granted.

Be gentle with yourself. Think less and feel more. Be as happy as you can. You only have this moment.

—DAN MILLMAN

Add to your to-do list: *Give myself a break.*

> Health is a state of body. Wellness is a state of being.
>
> —*J. Stanford*

Media mogul and queen of inspiration Oprah Winfrey kicked off a wellness journey tour in 2020 to help people define what being well actually means for them. She was kind enough to join Jenna and me—and a studio full of her fans—to talk about achieving wellness. I loved her question to all of us: "What is the real reason you're here? What is the special gift you were given to offer others?" To raise children? To help people? Feeling fulfilled may happen when we realize we're *actually* doing the things that make us happy and whole. In the search for physical and emotional health, Oprah emphasized that perfection isn't the goal; wholeness is the goal. We need to set "the ideal" for ourselves and work toward reaching and maintaining that. "If you name it, then claim it," she said. Love that! Don't wait for your best life to show up. It's waiting on *you* to define it, so you can begin to work toward it.

You don't need someone to complete you. You only need someone to accept you completely.

Thanks, honey. I know my list of flaws and so do you . . . but you still love me.

> My favorite machine at the gym is the vending machine.
>
> —*Caroline Rhea*

Haley weighs about thirty-five pounds, so I bought a weight of that poundage to strengthen my arms. I want to be able to pick her up and put her down dozens of times a day without getting fatigued. Great plan, right? Well, I just walked past it for the thousandth time. *There's that thing I'm supposed to be hoisting right now.* It's actually in the way and I should move it, but I keep hoping . . . one day . . .

Proximity breeds empathy.

When protests—both peaceful and violent—broke out across our nation following the death of African American George Floyd, we invited Rabbi Steve Leder and Bishop Kenneth Ulmer to *Today*. The two lead "sister" congregations in Los Angeles and have been friends for many years. During our conversation, Bishop Ulmer referenced a beautiful quote that one of his friends often shares: "Proximity breeds empathy." That rang so true to me. The closer we are to someone else's daily experience, the more we understand their perspective and they, ours. The bishop, who's African American, said that while he and the rabbi don't always agree, their long-term friendship provides a high level of respect and caring. In fact, the bishop told Rabbi Leder that while he may not have known it, his was the very first call he received when the violent protests began. In the middle of a very unsettling night, Rabbi Leder was making sure his old friend was all right.

> Your body is your most priceless possession; you've got to take care of it. —*Jack LaLanne*

Some of the funniest posts during the COVID-19 crisis addressed the *lack* of care we took of our bodies. People joked that they were eating every day as if headed to the electric chair, or that their jeans had a "come to Jesus" meeting with them. How did you do? I attempted to jog wearing a mask but felt like I was suffocating. A tub of caramel popcorn didn't stand a chance with me in the room. Clearly, a lot of us ate and drank our feelings away during such a stressful time.

> Don't let what you cannot do interfere with what you can do.
>
> —*John Wooden*

NBC's Bobbie Thomas is an expert on beauty, inside and out. There's some sort of lightness of being about her, a grace that glows. I love Bobbie's positive attitude, which is why I'm not surprised she shared a version of this quote when talking about her journey with her husband, Michael. At forty, he'd suffered a stroke, and now, one year later, Bobbie was overjoyed to report that he was walking with assistance, and they were coping well during the pandemic. "The past year has really helped us with the skills that we're using now," she said. "We're really focused lately on what we have and what we can do versus what we can't." Bobbie said their four-year-old son, Miles, has developed an empathetic heart by simply watching the family manage Michael's recovery. One night, when they asked him about the bright spot in his day, he said, "My high was seeing how strong Daddy is. I'm so proud of him." Of all the conversations I've had with Bobbie about beauty, that one was *the* most beautiful.

Poetry is the lifeblood of rebellion, revolution, and the raising of awareness.　　　　　　　　　　—*Alice Walker*

Yes. Powerful, peaceful words.

The day the Lord created hope was
probably the same day he
created spring.

—BERNARD WILLIAMS

Easter 2020 was anything but traditional. The COVID-19 pandemic prevented church gatherings, so worshipers turned to cyber sermons, eager for comfort. I loved the message I heard during the service I watched: that we should view being alone during the crisis as an act of love; we were protecting each other. Despite the crisis, Easter was extra special for our family because Hope turned one. Like millions of others, we "Brady Bunched" on Zoom, singing "Happy Birthday" and sharing Easter greetings. My friend and driver Eddie surprised my girls and me with a special message on the sidewalk: a heart drawn in chalk with "HAPPY EASTER" written above it. Inside the heart he wrote, "Haley, Hope, Mom, Dad, love, peace, joy." And Eddie donned a blue Cookie Monster onesie and an Elmo shirt as a treat for Haley and Hope! What a good egg. Small kindnesses like Eddie's meant so much to me during those difficult days, as I'm sure they did to you.

Sharing food with another human being is an intimate act that should not be indulged in lightly.   —*M.F.K. Fisher*

I agree, and I wish I was better at savoring a meal. Instead, I attack food and celebrate the experience with spirited chewing. (A fellow passenger on a plane once asked me to lay off the wad of gum I was working with vigor. Sorry!) Joel, on the other hand, is a very delicate eater. Somehow, he sees the meal as secondary to the conversation. He'll take a bite, put down his fork, and quietly chew before continuing to chat. Even Hope is a more refined eater than I am, eating one green pea at a time off of her plate. Who knows what my deal is. I've tried to slow down but seem to always revert back to inhaling a meal. I'll keep working on it. #slowtheforkdown

> Feeling gratitude and not expressing it is like wrapping a present and not giving it. —*William Arthur Ward*

I've dog-eared and underlined the heck out of a book I carry around with me, written by American rabbi and scholar Steve Leder. He's a frequent guest on *Today*, and I find him full of comforting wisdom. In *More Beautiful Than Before: How Suffering Transforms Us*, Rabbi Leder shares an idea from psychologist Martin Seligman that packs a poignant punch and requires very little effort. First, think of someone who's changed your life in an enormously important way. Then, write about three hundred words you'd like to say to express your thanks. Here's the most important part: Call that person and ask to stop by. If they agree, show up for what Seligman calls a "gratitude visit" and read your testimonial face-to-face. Rabbi Leder says presenting thoughts out loud to someone is twice as powerful as that person's simply reading those same thoughts by themself. I have to agree! Imagine someone calling you—or you making the call—and asking: "I need five minutes to say thank you . . . will you listen?" Of course!

If a family has an old person in it, it possesses a jewel.

—*Chinese proverb*

That's what made it so hard for many families during the COVID-19 crisis, which stole our jewels for months and even forever. Oh, to hug our parents and grandparents! We so missed all of the vulnerable, lovable people in our lives, and they missed us. Windowpanes allowed us to see one another and blow kisses—phones, too—but never again will we take a bear hug with our seniors for granted.

> Don't be pushed around by the fears in your mind. Be led
> by the dreams in your heart.   —*Roy T. Bennett*

I can't imagine the fear one mom must have battled back to leave her children and join the health care force in New York City, the epicenter of the pandemic. One morning, as I sat on set, I noticed a woman in scrubs outside the window. She was easy to spot with the typically jam-packed plaza now void of people, all sheltering at home. I could only see this person's eyes and her sign, which read: "Amelia, Anthony, Charlotte," along with a paw print with the name "Maddie" beside it. She'd also written, "I miss you! Love, Mom." Next to a drawing of a house, she'd added, "I'll be home soon. You are ALL my sunshine." Moved by her sacrifice, I quickly wrote my cell phone number on a piece of script paper and held it up toward her. When she called, I learned her name was Natalie and she'd flown in from Atlanta to help our city. What a special person! We took a shot of her live on the air, and Mommy got to wave to the family she missed so much.

True intimacy is a state in which nothing exists between two people; no space, no inhibitions and no lies.

—*Ranata Suzuki*

In 2020, Jenna and I interviewed sex therapist Dr. Tiffanie Henry about the challenge of nurturing intimacy in romantic relationships. Dr. Tiff said low sexual desire or a discrepancy in desire is the number one issue she addresses with couples. Talking about getting busy on live television can be awkward, so I kept my own relationship off the table. When I told Dr. Tiff I have a friend who says if your man wants to have sex, try never to say no, she made a good point: "I'm never going to pooh-pooh what works in another woman's house, but it doesn't necessarily work in mine." I think that's right. Sure, it's normal to wonder how other people manage intimacy, but Dr. Tiff said it's always more effective to sit down with your own partner and let them know what you need and want—or don't want—in the bedroom. She also dropped a statistic that may relieve or overwhelm you: The average American couple is having sex once a week.

If a woman says, "Do what you want," DO NOT do what you want. Stand still, don't blink, don't answer, don't even breathe. Just play dead.

Oh yes . . . those tricky dynamics in relationships. During the cramped quarters of COVID-19, spouses and partners everywhere dealt with being in close range all day long, uncharted and often undesirable territory. A marriage and family therapist on *Today* offered advice for couples navigating the stay-at-home effort. He said that because we were outside of our typical routines and were anxious, we internalized everything, which disconnected us as partners. After the show, I talked with one of our studio cameramen, and it was clear to me that he didn't need *any* suggestions. Rope said that during the quarantine, he asked his wife to get ready for a date night while he transformed their basement into a bar, complete with home-cooked chicken wings, sliders, and cold beer. He set up a card table and covered it with a linen tablecloth. When he showed me the photo of those two sitting next to each other at "the bar," smiling, I loved Rope even more.

Be fearless in the pursuit of what sets your soul on fire.

I can truly relate to Anderson Cooper's astonishment at saying out loud, "I have a son." I felt the same surreal and completely fulfilling emotion when a woman asked me if I had children. "I have a daughter," I said, beaming. Astounding! In May 2020, Anderson welcomed his son's birth by a surrogate, calling the experience "an extraordinary blessing" in his Instagram baby announcement. Anderson wrote that Wyatt Morgan Cooper is named after his father, who died when Anderson was ten. I just know your soul is on fire for that child, Anderson. Congratulations, and yes, *you* have a son.

Difficult roads often lead to beautiful destinations.

—*Zig Ziglar*

If you're traveling a difficult road right now, may it soon turn into the Yellow Brick Road. Keep going!

My life is my message. —*Mahatma Gandhi*

What a simple way to make us think about our life's message. What does your life have to say?

With the new day comes new strength and new thoughts.

—ELEANOR ROOSEVELT

Well, that just turned my yawn into a roar!

> It's your road, and yours alone. Others may walk it with you, but no one can walk it for you. —*Rumi*

I thought former First Lady Michelle Obama offered a great reminder during her appearance on Oprah's 2020 Vision Tour. She talked about a phrase she shares with her daughters, "Walk *your* walk." You be you. Michelle said we often compare ourselves to others, but even though it may seem like someone else is doing better than we are, it's not productive to focus on anyone but ourselves. She offered the example of taking challenging, long hikes during a retreat. "I always found that when I was not enjoying my walk, I was comparing my walk to someone else in the group," she said. "I had to sort of start telling myself, *Stop comparing yourself to the person walking ahead of you or behind you. Walk your walk.*" I think social media makes it easy to feel less than or behind or unpopular. Michelle's message of defining our own pace and defining what makes us happy is important. As you head out the door today, walk *your* walk. You're gonna get it done *your* way!

When it rains look for rainbows, when it's dark look for stars.

In an effort to do their part, so many people looked for their sewing machines during the COVID crisis. Avid sewers already had theirs set up, ready to go. Others blew dust off their machines, energized to rediscover the comforting feel of needle and thread meeting fabric. How moving it was to see all the Singers and Brothers set up on kitchen tables and in sewing nooks. Americans worked overtime to create masks for neighbors, health care workers, and people across the country . . . by the hundreds and thousands. We wanted to do *something* to help! I loved the images of elders sewing with young kids who were either learning to sew or soaking up tips from a seasoned pro. I don't know how to sew, which made me marvel even more at the skills of so many who made it look easy. Creativity was off the charts, too, with crafters cutting up everything from tablecloths to sports jerseys. During that challenging time, the whir of a sewing machine became the sound of support and survival.

> Always walk through life as if you have something new to learn and you will.
>
> —*Vernon Howard*

This quote is so my mom, who's always eager to learn something new. Today is her birthday, and in 2020 it was a weird one, due to the pandemic. Normally, we celebrate her big day together; always have. Decades ago, when my mom was teaching a class at the University of Oklahoma, my sister, Hala; brother, Adel; and I flew in as a surprise for her birthday. We hadn't missed one since, until COVID-19 forced us to. For her safety, she stayed at home by herself, but she wasn't alone. Adel and his family showed up with cupcakes and sang to her, keeping their distance. Later in the day, Hala joined in a family Zoom session from Dubai, and my mom got dressed up for the call! So cute. I also sent her a video with Haley singing "Happy Birthday" wearing her little purple glasses. I told her we couldn't wait to make her cake and showed her all the ingredients at the ready on the counter. Mom, I hope we never again miss a birthday together . . . side by side. We love you!

> To succeed in life, you need three things: a wishbone, a backbone and a funny bone. —*Reba McEntire*

I rarely overprepare for stuff, but this day was super special. Joel and I were officially adopting Haley and Hope via videoconference with a judge, so I spent twenty minutes getting my phone set up to record the big moment. The girls, Joel, and I were huddled together in front of the computer when the ceremony began, live. Everything unfolded like a scripted movie! Hope was clapping, Haley responded to the judge with "I'm ready!," and Joel and I were beaming. After we completed the adoption and said our goodbyes, I headed over to stop my cell phone from recording. Whaaaat??? I'd leaned the phone up against a vase but had accidentally pointed the camera toward it, not us! Joel: "Did we get it?" Me: "Oh, we got it." When I told him what happened, we broke out into hysterics! Ten minutes of a green vase! I love that Joel and I have lived long enough to know what a real problem is and that this wasn't one.

Surround yourself with people who are going to lift you higher.

—OPRAH WINFREY

And return the favor!

> After all of this is over, all that will really matter is how we treated each other.

We call our lovable and talented *Today* photographer Nathan Congleton "Photo Nate." On the day I posted this quote on Instagram, NBC producers decided to use some of Nate's beautiful images to create a video of New Yorkers thanking their COVID-19 warriors on the front lines of the battle. Across the city at seven o'clock each evening, people leaned out of windows and stood on fire escapes in a unified effort to create a "symphony of appreciation." Nate captured the many ways neighbors made noise, using pot lids as cymbals, ringing cowbells, taking wooden spoons to iron skillets and ice buckets, clapping their hands. One of my favorite shots is of New York City firefighters surprising nurses with overflowing Easter baskets. Thank you, Nate. Your many and moving photos will always remind us not only how grateful we were for our heroes, but that we took the time to say thank you.

> Trust the magic of new beginnings.　　*—Meister Eckhart*

I posted this on the first day of a new professional adventure for Jenna and me. Our hour of *Today* was now adding a studio audience to the mix on Thursdays and Fridays. Wow—that first show was magic! We walked out to a sea of pink and red pom-poms and excited folks eager to give out hugs. Special surprises included singer Meghan Trainor (who we had been told couldn't make it), our handsome guys Henry and Joel, and a visit from our beautiful kids. DJ Mad Marj rocked the house, and viewers from around the country we'd surprised with tickets joined us for a fun game on set. People at home and in the audience probably thought Jenna and I were nuts, crying throughout the program. I think we were so emotional because we'd been envisioning what the show could be, and finally, our new adventure was unfolding right before our eyes. How grateful we are for all of the people who showed up that first day, and for all the fun memories to come . . . with friends.

Stressed spelled backward is desserts. Coincidence? I think not!

We needed all the laughter we could get during the COVID-19 crisis; it was medicine. One of my favorite posts poked fun at our weeks of collective stress eating:

> So, after this quarantine . . . will the producers of *My 600-lb Life* just find me . . . or do I call them . . . or how will this work?

The world will say to you: We need to end racism. Start by healing it in your own family.

The world will say to you: How do we speak to bias and bigotry? Start by having the first conversation at your own kitchen table.

The world will say to you: There is too much hate. Devote yourself to love. Love yourself so much that you can love others without barriers and without judgment.

—*Cleo Wade*

This sure sounds like a good start.

> The less I needed, the better I felt.   —*Charles Bukowski*

My dear friend Jennifer Miller is someone who, unlike me with my frequently chipped nail polish, is diligent about scheduling regular maintenance on her nails; her hair, too. When all of our routines were interrupted by the stay-at-home protocol during the pandemic, many of us—including Jen—realized we might never go back to our old habits. Jen said both her hair and her nails were now healthier! I had the same experience with Haley's schedule. Before the shutdown, we were running from one activity to the next. Swim class, music class, soccer. But, stuck at home, Haley's imagination blossomed. One day she handed me a pretend pizza for a pretend birthday party with her imaginary friend. "Caca boom boom's here, Mommy." Huh? "Okay, honey, let her in." Most of the time, she didn't even need toys to play with; life became simpler. Did you experience the same thing? I think those unprecedented times truly redefined "necessities" for many of us.

Sometimes, you just need a break. In a beautiful place. Alone. To figure everything out.

Even if it's just a few minutes lying on your back in the grass looking up at the stars. Fireflies blinking would be nice, too.

In three words I can sum up
everything I learned about life:
it goes on.

—ROBERT FROST

Simple. True. Comforting.

HK

> I didn't lose the gold, I won the silver. —*Michelle Kwan*

In 1998, figure skater Michelle Kwan appeared on *The Tonight Show with Jay Leno*. Eleven-year-old Jonathan Van Ness was watching. Now a cast member of the Netflix show *Queer Eye*, Jonathan told me how moved he was by Michelle's response to being asked about losing the gold medal at the Nagano games. "She said, 'I didn't lose the gold, I won the silver,'" he recalled. "It taught me to accept what is and be excited for what is." Jonathan said that as a young boy, he learned that a so-called loss was nothing of the sort. "When is an Olympic silver medal a disappointment? It was the most incredible achievement ever!" Now friends with Michelle, Jonathan says her tenacity still motivates him. "It just made me want to learn as much as I can about everything I'm passionate about." And that includes Jonathan's recent efforts at figure skating and gymnastics. (Nice videos, Jonathan! You're quite accomplished at both!)

I love you not only for what you are, but for what I am when I am with you. —*Elizabeth Barrett Browning*

The right one brings out the best version of yourself!

For the rest of my life I will search for moments full of you.

A concerned daughter in Louisiana reached out to me about her mother, Carolyn, whom she called "the most thoughtful and generous person." For the first time in fifty-one years, Christy Reeves said her mom would be celebrating her birthday without her beloved husband, who had died the past summer. In addition to that heartbreak, the pandemic required Carolyn to spend her seventy-fourth birthday indoors, where she'd been cooped up for seven weeks. As a surprise, Jenna and I made a video call to Carolyn live on the air . . . and she picked up! Once she figured out who was calling, her reaction was priceless: "Oh, you're going to make me cry." What a sweetheart. After we assured Carolyn she was not alone, we suggested she go to the door. Gathered outside with a cake and balloons were her daughters and granddaughters! We were all emotional, hoping in some way that family and a simple phone call could heal a tiny patch of Carolyn's broken heart.

> The moment you accept responsibility for EVERYTHING in your life is the moment you gain the power to change ANYTHING in your life. —*Hal Elrod*

When *Black-ish* actress Tracee Ellis Ross joined Oprah onstage during Oprah's 2020 Vision Tour, I watched the interview twice. I soaked up Tracee's insights about getting to know herself and what she wants. "As I've gotten older, I've become more myself," she said. "And the more I am myself, the more my life looks like me—not the same as anyone else's." I love that connection—be authentically you and your best life will follow. Tracee also made it clear that she's in charge of her decisions. "I, like many of us, was taught to grow up dreaming of my wedding, not of my life," she said. "I spent many years dreaming of my wedding, and also waiting to be chosen. But here's the thing: I'm the chooser." I'm the chooser! Powerful, right? Perhaps today keep in mind these four words that Tracee wrote in her journal: "My life is mine."

> Reality is a question of perspective.   —*Salman Rushdie*

Consider all that a person born in 1900 endured.

14th birthday: World War I begins
18th birthday: World War I ends, Spanish Flu pandemic begins
20th birthday: Spanish Flu ends, killing 100 million people
29th birthday: Great Depression begins, Dust Bowl begins
36th birthday: Great Depression and Dust Bowl end
39th birthday: WWII begins
41st birthday: US fully pulled into WWII
45th birthday: WWII ends, killing 75 million people
50th birthday: Korean War begins and ends three years later
55th birthday: Vietnam War begins
75th birthday: Vietnam War ends

A child born in 1985 may not realize that his eighty-five-year-old grandparent survived so much.

Everything in your life is
a reflection of a choice you
have made. If you want
a different result, make
a different choice.

Um, that sounds reasonable, right? The power of choice.

> Those who are happiest are those who do the most for others.   —*Booker T. Washington*

In a *New York* magazine article, Congressman John Lewis offered hope at a time when our country was erupting with protests and heated discussions about race relations following the death of George Floyd. Eighty years old at the time of the interview, Lewis grew up in an Alabama sharecropping family, spent his early adulthood as a civil rights activist, and had served as a Georgia congressman since 1987. Suffering from stage-four pancreatic cancer, he maintained a positive outlook on the future of our nation and the world. "I've come in contact with people who feel inspired. They've just never been along in a protest, and they decided to march with their children and their grandchildren and great-grandchildren," he said. "They're helping to educate and inspire another generation of activists." He encouraged this mindset. "We're one family. We all live in the same house. Not just an American house but the world house. As Dr. King said over and over again, 'We must learn to live together as brothers and sisters. If not, we will perish as fools.'"

> We never get over great losses; we absorb them, and they
> carve us into different, often kinder creatures.
>
> —*Gail Caldwell*

In her weekly online newsletter, *Sunday Paper*, Maria Shriver hoped for us all to become kinder creatures during and following the horrific pandemic. The last paragraph is so meaningful for any time in our lives that I wanted to offer it here, with Maria's suggesting that we ask ourselves just who we will be when we grow up:

As we ponder it, may we take comfort in this: while the future may feel uncertain, what will always be certain and essential is our love. The love I have for myself. The love I have for my family and friends. The love I have for you, even though I may not know you personally. It is essential. Yes it is. Love is the one essential ingredient that our world cannot move forward without. Not now. Not anymore.

> Call it a clan, call it a network, call it a tribe, call it a family. Whatever you call it, whoever you are, you need one.
>
> —*Jane Howard*

My dear friend Janie told me her mother always used to tell her sisters and her, "Blood is thicker than water." A bit confusing, the phrase was Mom's way of encouraging them to always reserve their highest loyalty for each other. The message was a good one, as Janie and her sisters have been through a lot together, serving as each other's unwavering support system through every challenge. I think that's why this quote encourages us to find our [fill in the blank]. We need people in our life who will always have our back.

> The craving for "the return of the day," which the sick so constantly evince, is generally nothing but the desire for light.
>
> —*Florence Nightingale*

I don't think National Nurses Day will get left behind anymore on the "holiday importance" scale. The observance is today, and for literally millions of reasons, our nation can never fully convey the admiration we feel for nurses and the entire medical community. During the COVID-19 pandemic, our heroes in scrubs *were* the light for all of us, whether we were sick or healthy—the light, the hope, the comfort. We prayed for them, cheered for them, fed them, turned city lights blue for them—nothing was enough. Because families understandably could not visit their loved ones in the hospital, brave nurses stood in for us . . . holding up phones so we could say "I love you," even holding the hands of our dying beloveds. Exhausted nurses were Americans' extended family, all the while worrying about and missing their own. Then and now, these courageous souls are our lifelines. We love you, nurses, even more than we already did. Our gratitude is as big as your hearts.

Family is belonging to and believing in each other.

For a decade now, the Gerber baby food company has selected a baby spokesperson from photos sent in by proud parents. In 2020, a little girl named Magnolia Earl was chosen, the first adopted child to represent the brand. I was so moved watching the Earl family react to the honor, as they learned on *Today* that their little girl was not just a finalist but indeed the winner. Courtney Earl, Magnolia's mom, shared what the historic decision meant to her family, as little Magnolia cooed and wriggled around in her dad's lap. "It means that when people see our families, or you see a family that doesn't necessarily match," Courtney said, "that you don't have to question the belonging of anybody in that family." The California couple has two other daughters, twelve and eight, the younger daughter also adopted. Russell Earl lovingly added, "What does Mommy say? Mommy always says, 'A family is built on love.' We may all look different," he said, "but we're one family." Just beautiful. Congratulations, Magnolia!

Some days I wish
I could go back in life,
not to change things,
just to feel a few things twice.

Moments with my dad.

> My mother—she is beautiful, softened at the edges and tempered with a spine of steel. I want to grow old and be like her.
>
> —*Jodi Picoult*

I talk to my mother every day on the phone and see her as often as I can—at least once a month. She's not just my mom, she's one of my best friends. During the COVID-19 crisis, my mom stayed at home or at the beach by herself for weeks. Already the most positive person I know, she kept up her sunny outlook every day, taking selfies to share with me what she was up to. "Look at me by the water!" she'd text, showing herself safely separated from anybody else. She sent pictures of the mug I'd sent her filled with coffee . . . everyday stuff. Boy, I sure missed seeing her in person during that stretch, as I know you did your loved ones. FaceTime was a lifesaver, right? Nothing made my mom happier than to see my girls and to talk with them on her phone. If anything positive came out of that isolation, perhaps it was that we realized how lucky we are when we can bear-hug the people we love. Happy Mother's Day, Mom. I love you.

> Honesty and transparency make you vulnerable. Be honest and transparent anyway. —*Saint Teresa of Calcutta*

In a 2020 newspaper interview, actor Ben Affleck discussed his struggles with alcohol addiction. As Jenna and I talked on-air about how we admired his honesty, Jenna shared a story about a conversation she'd had with her father, former president George W. Bush. Jenna said that when she was in her early twenties, her dad, an alcoholic, asked her to go for a walk. "He said to me, 'I just want to talk to you about drinking. I found in my own life that it got in the way of the things that mattered most, and I just want you to know that it can.'" Jenna recalled the walk vividly and said her dad's honesty now serves as a model for how she wants to parent—with transparency and candor. Boy, I respect her father's courage to have what was surely a difficult conversation. I'm trying to be better about talking through issues I may have with someone instead of pushing those feelings aside. I've found that while the process can be uncomfortable, the end result is *so* freeing.

Be brave. Take risks. Nothing can substitute experience.

—*Paulo Coelho*

Some say, "Fake it 'til you make it," and I think that's just another way of encouraging us to dive in and experience things so we learn and grow along the way.

> Opportunities to find deeper powers within ourselves
> come when life seems most challenging.
>
> —*Joseph Campbell*

I'm entirely sure that I'm not the first woman to wish she were Tiffany Haddish's BFF. When I interviewed her in January 2019, she was costarring in the movie *Like a Boss*. Tiffany is so funny and vulnerable at the same time that you just want to know everything about her life and her light. She sparkles! You'd never guess that her childhood experiences in South Central Los Angeles were grim, with years spent in the foster care system and a stint living in her car following high school. Still, through humor and positive thinking, Tiffany refused to let her past define her. By "working her butt off" and "speaking things into existence," she became a successful stand-up comedian and a multi-award-winning actress. When I watched a video of her accepting a 2018 *Essence* award, I admired her shout-out to longtime friends seated in front of her. "Table twenty-four!" she yelled. Tiffany also hit up her friend Rev. "Rev, look at us now, Rev!" She then recognized the rest of her loyal pals, grateful they've been by her side through every challenge.

Time flies whether you're having fun or not.
The choice is yours.

Have some fun today!

> If there is a heaven for me, I'm sure there is a beach attached to it.
> —*Jimmy Buffett*

Already a cool dude, Jimmy Buffett proved not only how much he loves his fans (called "Parrot Heads") but also how grateful he was to health care workers during the coronavirus crisis. Jimmy said on *Today* that his gratitude comes from firsthand experience. "I've had a couple of near misses when I was in the hands of first responders and wonderful health care people," he explained, "so it comes from the heart for me." Because Jimmy knows his music is often played in operating and emergency rooms as a pick-me-up, he reached out to health care workers in "Parrot Clubs" and arranged to perform online concerts for them every Friday night. At the end of our live interview with Jimmy, he surprised a respiratory therapist who left her family in Tennessee to help in New York City. When he awarded her a well-deserved vacation at one of his Margaritaville resorts, Gena Bryant's reaction was priceless! Her arms raised and head thrown back, she yelled, "Thank yooou!" We could all feel how much she—and all frontline workers—needed a getaway.

> Music is an outburst of the soul. —*Frederick Delius*

When Mariah Carey shared with *Billboard* that she quizzes her kids on which iconic artists sing what songs, Jenna and I began talking about our own children and the impact music has in their lives. Jenna shared that her mother's love of music meant that records were always playing in the house, and Mom even took her and her sister to a Paul Simon concert when they were in first grade! I try to share my passion for music with Haley and Hope, although at Haley's age we're often listening to Super Simple Songs and "Baby Shark" on repeat. I created a "Happy" playlist for Haley that includes songs like Pharrell's "Happy" and Bobby McFerrin's "Don't Worry, Be Happy." Some of my other favorites are throwbacks, like "It's a Sunshine Day" from the *Brady Bunch* series. Because of that song, Haley sings, "I think I'll go for a walk outside now," whenever we head outside! We'll see if music lights them up in years to come. In the meantime, I'll just keep hitting the "play" button.

If you don't risk anything, you risk even more.

—*Erica Jong*

Countless Americans risked their lives to save others during the COVID-19 crisis. Among so many others: drivers of buses, trucks, and ride services; grocery workers; mail, package, and food deliverers; restaurant staff; first responders; veterinarians; pharmacists; custodians; flight crews; and of course, health care workers, who so kindly but urgently asked us to do our part. I was moved by the message so many sent as a masked group, holding up handwritten signs in their gloved hands: "WE STAY AT WORK FOR YOU . . . PLEASE STAY AT HOME FOR US!!!"

May grace meet you where you are and take you where you want to go.

I decided to punch the thesaurus button in Microsoft Word for "grace." It's such a lovely word, filled with hope for how we might best carry ourselves during difficult times. Here are the close friends of grace, and may we be inspired by them as we make our way through the day:

poise
kindness
mercy
charity
decency
blessing

> You don't manifest dreams without taking chances.
>
> —*Stephen Richards*

I've given several of my grown-up friends a particular children's book because to me, it's a message for anyone—kids and adults. *What Do You Do with a Chance?* explores a child's journey through being presented with chances. What happens when you ignore a chance? Or when you take a chance and fail? We do a dance with chances our whole lives, choosing . . . wondering . . . regretting. At this very moment, someone is debating whether to remain a wallflower or cut a rug. I took a big chance leaving my beloved New Orleans to take a job at NBC in New York, and I was terrified. But in the end, I made the right decision. I haven't always, but I've tried to err on the side of yes, especially after breast cancer laser-focused my perspective on living. I picture my kids when I read that book, holding tight to a big, beautiful chance with the wind in their hair and a smile on their face. And me, looking up, cheering them on.

There is virtue in work and there is virtue in rest. Use both and overlook neither.

—ALAN COHEN

I've heard "Work hard, play hard," but I'd like to tack on "rest hard."

If we believe that tomorrow will be better, we can bear a hardship today.   —*Thich Nhat Hanh*

Optimism 101.

A candle loses nothing by lighting another candle.

—*James Keller*

Spread your light. It always reflects back and warms our soul.

> When someone else's happiness is your happiness, that
> is love.   —*Lana Del Rey*

Did you see the video of the proud dad who lost his mind when his son hit a home run? Wow! If you need a smile today, Google "watch this dad react when his son hits a homer over the fence." We aired the video as a "Morning Boost" and watched with glee as a toddler's father pitched to the little guy—decked out in full uniform and helmet—at their local ballpark. Bam! The pint-sized hitter rips one over the fence for an HR! Apparently, Dad was practicing with his son for a month, perfecting his swing. Watching this momentous achievement sends Coach into happiness overload, as he jumps up and down, arms raised in victory, twirling around the field yelling, "YOU DID IT! YEAAAAH!" The boy races around the bases, giggling, as Dad bounces up and down like a pogo stick, meeting his son at home plate for a high five and a bear hug. I mean, who needs a stand full of fans? What a beautiful reaction, Dad. That is love.

One way to get the most out of life is to look upon it as an adventure.   —*William Feather*

I like that. An adventure with ups and downs, but still . . . an adventure.

> An open heart is an open mind.
>
> —*The Fourteenth Dalai Lama*

I'm a sign person; I look for signs when I'm wondering about big stuff. Remember the heartbreaking photo of a toddler covered in blood and dust during the war in Syria? I considered that a sign confirming I should adopt a baby. When I was writing in my journal about whether Joel and I should adopt a third child, I watched my pen ask and answer questions:

Do we have enough love? Yes.
Do we have enough time? Yes.
Would another child enhance our family? Yes.

I wondered if all those yeses were signs, looking up at me from the page. Because Joel and I are older parents, I just want to make sure my kids have someone to hold their hand, forever. Haley and Hope have each other . . . but perhaps by the time this is in print they'll have another set of hands to hold and be held by. We'll see. Whatever is meant to be, I'm beyond happy. And endlessly grateful.

> Clutter is nothing more than postponed decisions.
>
> —*Barbara Hemphill*

Whenever Martha Stewart comes to *Today*, I always admire her tips on cooking and decorating, but in my mind I'm thinking, *I'll never do that*. I know myself! At the start of one year, she came to set with a new book about organizing your home. Martha talked about how her kitchen is "organized to the nth degree." Mine is organized to the n(othing)th degree, counters covered with kid gear, mail, and stuff underneath other stuff. When I lived in New Orleans, my news director came into my apartment and was clearly jarred by the sight of cabinets and drawers left open, clothes strewn everywhere. When he described the scene to a coworker, he said, "It looked like there were signs of a struggle." Still does, Joe. I'm a lost cause, but you may be up for Martha's four organizational tips:

1. Use drawer dividers in the kitchen
2. Put kitchen utensils in a crock on the counter
3. Use baskets and folders to organize mail and paperwork
4. Use monthly, weekly, and daily planners

You can't go back and make a new start, but you can start right now and make a brand new ending.

—*James R. Sherman*

This is so powerful. Reading your life story is not proactive. Writing it is.

There are shortcuts to happiness, and dancing is one of them.
—Vicki Baum

Everybody has their jam, and Hope's includes the Blanco Brown song "The Git Up." She holds my hands and we slide to the left, then slide to the right. She's totally into it! Hope *loves* to dance, especially to any song with a beat that makes her bounce or jump up and down. Whenever a peppy song ends, she looks up at me like, "Hurry up and hit 'play' again, Mommy!"

> Forget not that the earth delights to feel your bare feet and
> the winds long to play with your hair.   —*Kahlil Gibran*

In a rare radio interview, the Duchess of Cambridge spoke about her experiences as a child and now a mother of three. A British personality hosted the podcast, which offered Kate Middleton a chance to talk about her initiative to help parents maximize their children's early development. I loved what she said about her own upbringing: "I had an amazing granny who devoted a lot of time to us, playing with us, doing arts and crafts and going to the greenhouse to do gardening, and cooking with us." The duchess also spoke about the importance of kids' spending time outdoors, which I try to do as often as possible with mine, even if it's for a short walk or stroll. It sure was nice to hear some thoughts from Kate. Her voice is so seldom heard that I think it makes us lean in more when she speaks. By the way, Duchess, your kids are beautiful!

> You must tell yourself, "No matter how hard it is, or how hard it gets, I'm going to make it." —*Les Brown*

Their wings must have been tucked inside their personal protective equipment. I just had to post a video of two Barcelona hospital workers—angels—serenading an elderly woman who was unable to move for thirty days, battling COVID-19 in the intensive care unit. Staff captured the moment when two physiotherapists who'd donned PPE from head to toe had the patient up and moving, one slow-dancing with her, the other swaying to the music. Somehow, the IV lines and beeping machines disappeared and the trio was on a Spanish piazza at dusk, enjoying the evening beside a bistro. Heartwarming doesn't begin to describe the images. I agree with what someone posted about the video: "Love wins."

PS: Happy birthday, Dad!

It is a happy talent to know how to play.

—*Ralph Waldo Emerson*

Jimmy Fallon is as kind as he is talented. I *love* Jimmy. During the pandemic, we all got to see an even more dear side of him, as he worked from home. Viewers got to meet his adorable daughters, six-year-old Winnie and Franny, five. While hosting *The Tonight Show*, Jimmy included the two cuties in his daily monologues, talking as the sisters did arts and crafts and snacked. He even let them help with his thank-you-note segments, one daughter holding charts, the other playing the "thank-you-note music" on an iPad. Jimmy's wife, Nancy, operated the camera, and joined him from time to time for "Ask the Fallons." The family dog, Gary, even shared in the fun. Oh, how we could all relate to the random outbursts, bouts of disinterest, and un-bridled giggling that make a house a home. Thanks for having that "show must go on" attitude, Jimmy. And your family is priceless!

We are forever indebted to those who have given their lives that we might be free. —*Ronald Reagan*

We all teared up on set one morning watching an awesome military reunion. (I think we do every single time we watch one!) A toddler named Tatum was at preschool clutching a "daddy doll" his mom had given him to ease the pain of missing his dad, who was serving overseas for a year with the US Air Force. As the three-year-old huddled in his teacher's lap clutching the doll, his adorable classmates sat in a row, listening. When the teacher asked Tatum what he would do if he saw his dad, he mumbled, "I don't know," his face buried in the doll. Then . . . the classroom door opens and in walks you-know-who! Tatum pops up and races toward his smiling dad. Dressed in his camouflage gear and boots, Michael scoops up Tatum and squeezes him tight. Of course Mom is on duty capturing the sweet moment on her camera phone. On this day and *every* day, we thank our military and their families for the many sacrifices they make—including the ultimate sacrifice—for our country. We love you!

Don't base your decisions on the advice of people who don't have to deal with the results.

So true. Pick your advisors wisely . . . ones with skin in the game.

> The true warrior isn't immune to fear. She fights in spite of it. —*Francesca Lia Block*

When B. K. Fulton, founding chairman and CEO of Soulidifly Productions, delivered the commencement address for Virginia Commonwealth University's da Vinci Center, he reminded students to never forget people on the margins, like the lesser-known female warriors. Here are a few:

Marie Van Brittan Brown: Invented the home security system in 1969 in response to the high level of crime in her Queens, New York, neighborhood.

Shirley Ann Jackson: The first black woman to earn a PhD from MIT. She headed up the team that developed the technology leading to the touchtone phone, caller ID, and call waiting.

Dr. Gladys West: Invented GPS and was inducted into the Space and Missile Pioneers Hall of Fame in 2018.

Being scared is part of being alive. Accept it. Walk through it.
—*Robin Sharma*

And don't be afraid to reach out for a hand to hold, if only for a few steps as you regain your footing.

More is lost by indecision than wrong decision. Indecision is the thief of opportunity. It will steal you blind.

—*Marcus Tullius Cicero*

Indecision is all that sand in the bottom of an hourglass. Is there something you need to decide?

> Music is the divine way to tell beautiful, poetic things to the heart.
>
> *—Pablo Casals*

I'm a huge fan of the country group Little Big Town. When Jenna and I took our guys to see them perform at Carnegie Hall, we were blown away by the magic of their signature sound inside that historic building. (We also loved seeing them wave—in midsong—to their kids sitting in the front row!) Karen Fairchild, Kimberly Schlapman, Phillip Sweet, and Jimi Westbrook have worked together for more than twenty years, and when they released their ninth album, *Nightfall*, they performed several songs on *Today* live from Orlando. The crowd went wild! I think LBT is beloved because of their genuine gratitude for their fans, and because of their musical range: one song makes you laugh, and the next one makes you weep. "The Daughters" is one of my favorites because the song's message is so positive for young girls. LBT, keep up the amazing work. We can't wait to soak up everything you have to share with us in the next twenty years!

True friends are always together in spirit.

Our besties are always tagging along with us, humming a beautiful tune in our heart.

HK

> There is no such thing as a perfect parent, so just be a
> real one.   —*Sue Atkins*

Things got *very* real for parents working from home during the
COVID-19 crisis. Many kept their senses of humor, but their sanity?
Not so much. I laughed out loud at many of the work-from-home
challenges posted on social media, some parents begging not to be
fired for off-putting kid sounds during conference calls, others de-
scribing the madness of trying to work as a child whispered, "Can
you hear me now?" in their ear.

The most romantic things are very small, kind gestures from people you love.

Don't you love when a little thing makes a big difference in your day? That happened to me when Joel did a little something for my mom. We'd traveled to the beach to celebrate Haley's third birthday, and on the day we were leaving, my mom walked downstairs to join us for coffee at seven o'clock in the morning. Our train didn't leave until eleven, but my mom likes to have her things in order well in advance. She said, "My bag's already packed. It just needs to be zipped up, and then I'm all ready." Now, that's my mom's way of saying, "Can you please go get it?" We all have things we like a certain way, right? Joel picked up on it and said, "Oh, I'll go get it now, Sami." And he did. I could tell my mom was so appreciative. I was, too. Thank you, honey, for the little kindness and for your big heart.

> It's scary to be vulnerable. We reach for our greatest need while risking our greatest pain. —*Danny Silk*

How interesting it was during the COVID-19 crisis to really see people's eyes. Because noses and mouths were hidden behind masks, our "windows to the soul" garnered all the attention. During such a surreal time, we were laser-focused on each other's eyes. Maybe you felt like I did: that even as we were seeing less of each other's faces, we were better able to see more of each other's pain, joy, fear . . . and love.

The best thing about telling the truth is that you don't have to remember what you said.

Exactly. Sir Walter Scott said it best when he wrote, "O, what a tangled web we weave when first we practice to deceive!"

June 11

Don't give someone the credit for holding you back. Give yourself the power in continuing to move forward.

—*Chris Burkmenn*

I had the good fortune in 2016 to watch, in person, the US Olympic gymnastics team compete in the summer games in Rio. Like me, the world was blown away by their gold medal performance. Just a few years later, we'd learn that many of the women were stronger than we could ever know, competing at the highest level while shouldering a dark secret. Gymnast Aly Raisman was one of the most insistent voices—often on *Today*—in the effort to reveal decades of physical abuse by the team doctor. She even braved sharing the room with him, testifying at his sentencing hearing. When Aly returned to *Today* in January 2020, she looked radiant, like a weight was lifting. She talked about taking up golf and gardening, and simply having fun. "I want people to know that my life is not perfect; there's no such thing as that. . . . I'm working a lot now on being okay, with some days having a tougher time." I think we can all relate to that, Aly. We love you. You are golden.

Life isn't about
finding yourself.
Life is about
creating yourself.

Why waste time searching? Take time today to create an even better version of yourself!

Respect yourself enough to say, "I deserve better."

A little girl we interviewed on *Today* felt that she and other kids deserved more from their crayon selection. Nine-year-old Bellen Woodard, a Virginia elementary school student, explained that when she was in third grade, classmates would ask her for the "skin color" crayon, which was labeled "peach." An African American, Bellen wondered why there was only one crayon to represent the way someone looked. "It just made me feel kinda disincluded," she said, "and like there is only one skin color, when there's more than one." Bellen decided that the "Bellen's More Than Peach" project would solve the problem. With two hundred dollars of her own money, she created coloring kits with crayons from Crayola's multicultural line and handed them out to her peers. Bellen's mom, Tosha, couldn't be more proud of her caring daughter. "This certainly is about far more than just the crayons," Tosha said. "It's about fostering a love of yourself and others, and being your best self." Way to go, Bellen! As we open our boxes of crayons, we'll open our minds to the variety of colors that represent our world.

> We rise by lifting others. —*Robert Ingersoll*

Ellen DeGeneres is both kind and hilarious. Whenever I'm with her, I feel comfortable and protected and ready for fun. Ellen creates that welcoming space for anyone who's with her. When I was on her show in January 2020, we talked about my engagement and adopting my second daughter, Hope. One minute I was crying, the next I was laughing hysterically at a surprise she had for me: a large poster of country singer Blake Shelton (my on-air crush) in case I had a bachelor-ette party. Actually, it was the rock-hard body of an unknown guy with Blake's head cut and pasted on the neck. Ahem . . . and the poster included a bull's-eye directly over the hot dude's family jewels. Hilarious! Ellen's humor is always on target. You bet I jammed that poster into the overhead bin on the flight home. Thanks for the love and laughs, Ellen. You're the absolute best.

I do not fix problems. I fix thinking. Then problems fix themselves.
                                        —*Louise L. Hay*

I suppose some problems *are* created by our mindset. Negativity certainly loves to invite its friends to the party: apathy, depression, pessimism, jealousy. Let's fix our thinking!

> Happiness, knowledge, not in another place but this place, not for another hour but this hour.   —*Walt Whitman*

I hope you feel as happy as I do that we're spending a moment together. This moment.

Being positive doesn't happen by chance. It's a decision.

—*Diamante Lavendar*

Olympic figure skater Scott Hamilton lights up a room like he lights up a skating rink. You just can't help but smile when you're with him. In February 2020, Scott talked on *Today* about his children's book, *Fritzy Finds a Hat.* Diagnosed multiple times with cancer, Scott decided to write a book to help kids understand how they can support a sick parent. Fritzy, the book's main character, knows his mom is going to lose her hair, so he decides to find her the perfect hat. "It's about empowering children to know they can make a difference in their family's lives." Scott said he learned to stay positive from his mother, who was diagnosed with cancer when he was sixteen years old. "She taught me how to go through cancer. . . . 'Oh, this is chemotherapy, I hate my hair . . . these wigs are so much easier.' . . . So, when I went through my cancer, it's like, 'All right, nobody's allowed in my room unless they make me laugh.'" What a guy. What a smile. You inspire us, Scott.

> I went inside myself, and decided to choose myself.
>
> —*Billy Porter*

I'm always struck by Billy Porter's positivity and light; Billy leads with his light. Actor and singer extraordinaire, Billy told me that for much of his life, he didn't allow himself to shine and instead shrunk to fit in. "For the first half of my life, that's all I did," he said. "I tried to mute myself, my truth, my personality." But during his thirties, Billy said everything in his world fell apart, and all that he was running from caught up with him. It was at rock bottom where he decided something had to change. "I just sat quietly, and I went inside myself," he explained, "and decided to choose myself. And it's all turned around." I think that's so powerful—to explore who we truly are and to say, "I choose me." Thank you, Billy, for unleashing your many gifts on and off the stage. Keep shining that bright light of yours!

Fear is only temporary. Regret lasts forever.

Better to go for it than go on and on someday about how you should have!

My father didn't tell me how to live; he lived, and let me watch him do it. —*Clarence Budington Kelland*

We have eight thousand coffee mugs in our house, but Joel only drinks out of one of them. "Where's my mug?" he'll ask. It's always in the dishwasher because he used it the previous morning. Haley and Hope made it for him, and it reads, "Good morning, Daddy. We love you so much." Their little handprints are also featured on the mug along with two hearts. What a sweet way for Daddy to start his day.

Not enough black women had a seat at the table, so I had to go and chop down that wood and build my own table.

—*Beyoncé*

Commencement speeches fire me up, and Queen Bey's was no exception. Via YouTube, she spoke to the class of 2020 across the nation about the importance of perseverance and unity. The superstar shared so many inspiring thoughts, including these: "Congratulations to the class of 2020. You have arrived here in the middle of a global crisis, a racial pandemic, and worldwide expression of outrage at the senseless killing of yet another unarmed black human being. And you still made it; we're so proud of you," she said in a video address. "We've seen that our collective hearts, when put to positive action, could start the wheels of change. Real change has started with you, this new generation of high school and college graduates who we celebrate today."

Little by little we let go of loss, but never of love.

We want to let go of pain because it drains us. Love fills us up.

> Stepping onto a brand-new path is difficult, but not more difficult than remaining in a situation, which is not nurturing to the whole woman.　　　　　　　　—*Maya Angelou*

A few months after moving to Nashville, Kathie Lee stopped by the *Today* set to chat with Jenna and me. (Of course she brought her own glass of wine.) She was beaming and funny and waving her arms around—the best of Kath. Always open with viewers about her life, she shared that her move south was due to a crippling loneliness. Kath said that while the Connecticut house where she and Frank Gifford had raised their children was wonderful, after Frank died in 2015 and Cody and Cassidy left home, the space was lifeless. "It went from being the most teeming, thrilling, joyful—all the dog sounds and kid sounds and smoke in the grill," she said, "and then it came to feel like a mortuary." Because Kathie Lee had a thirty-year history visiting and working in Nashville, she knew it was a place she'd feel alive again. And she was right! KLG is busier and more creative than ever. I'm so happy for you, Kath. You inspire any of us who hope to find the courage to create a new and exciting next chapter.

You're a diamond, dear.
They can't break you.

Sparkle today!

June 25

Stay close to people who feel like sunshine.

They are the ones who will be there for you on the rainy days.

I am enough, I have enough.

In the Netflix hit *Queer Eye*, cast members work as a team to lift up someone who needs a wardrobe or home makeover. The transformations are often emotional, as the "Fab Five" encourage and promote positive changes in people's lives. When I interviewed cast member Antoni Porowski, he shared that while it's easy to help others see their self-worth, he often struggles to acknowledge his own value. "I get into the trap of compare and despair. *I'm not working as hard as so-and-so; I'm not as successful as this person; and it's always, Am I doing well enough?*" Antoni explained. "It's a lot easier to be hard on myself than it is to congratulate myself." He said he's grateful to a friend who offered the quote "I am enough, I have enough," because it's helped him navigate his new role in the spotlight. Antoni will sit with the quote in the morning and repeat it to himself. "Imagine if we woke up every day and we actually believed that. Imagine how everything would change." *I am enough, I have enough.* Sure seems like it's worth a try, doesn't it?

> Joy is a decision, a really brave one, about how you are going to respond to life. —*Wess Stafford*

We typically think about joy washing over us in a moment of elation. I like how this quote encourages us to also think of joy as a mindset . . . our resting battle face.

Today, give thanks for those who have done you wrong. They've unknowingly made you strong.

Thanks, you-know-who.

What you believe, you receive.

When I sat down with several performers in the cast of the movie *Cats*, I was reminded what an extraordinary professional journey Jennifer Hudson has experienced. Consider the all-star cast of the film: Judi Dench, Idris Elba, Francesca Hayward, Taylor Swift . . . and a girl who placed seventh in the singing competition *American Idol*. In 2004, millions of Americans let Jennifer know that not only did she lose, but her talent ranked multiple slots behind the winner's. Years later, during a *Today* interview with Jennifer, I brought up the number-seven finish. Her answer was brief—something like, "I know, right?" There was no painful wince or hint of embarrassment. Why would there be? A string of extraordinary achievements followed: an Academy Award, Grammys, a Golden Globe, performances on Broadway, on television, and in movies. Boy, what a powerful reminder for any of us who've been passed over for a job . . . a team . . . a relationship. Surely Jennifer would agree—that was just life telling us it wasn't our time. The best is yet to come.

Someday, someone will walk into your life and make you realize why it never worked out with anyone else.

Just prior to their fortieth wedding anniversary, Phil Donahue and Marlo Thomas released a book about how to maintain a successful marriage. They've got some street cred! But in addition to discussing their own relationship, they interviewed forty celebrity couples about their marital journeys. From *What Makes a Marriage Last*, here are two pieces of advice shared by familiar folks:

+ Tape your arguments and listen back. You'll hear things you would have missed in the heated moment. (Ron and Cheryl Howard)
+ Always remember there is no plan B, no escape route in marriage. Work it out. (Kyra Sedgwick and Kevin Bacon)

> Courage isn't about knowing the path, it's about taking the
> first step.
> —*Katie Davis*

Some might consider this risky; others might feel relief that they don't have to have the whole ball of wax figured out. I'm definitely for taking the first step without all the answers. So far, I don't have any regrets, and my staircase is building itself!

My swimsuit told me to go to the gym today, but my sweat-pants were like, "Nah, girl, you're good."

Most days I drag myself to the gym or a spin class or outside for a run. I've never been someone who loves to work out, but I try to do it more often than not because it's good for me. Now, whenever my body feels blah, I think about a man named Lloyd Black we profiled on *Today*. *If Lloyd can do it, so can I.* Lloyd is a ninety-year-old retired principal who won "Member of the Month" at his Alabama gym. He said he joined because he was having trouble doing household chores and thought some exercise would help. Don't you love Lloyd already? His dedication to working out so inspired his fellow members, they presented him with the award. Here's the dearest part: Lloyd works out in coveralls in the winter and overalls in the summer. "I don't have much hips," he said. "If I get too active, I have trouble keeping my pants up." We feel you, Lloyd! Way to get it done. *If Lloyd can do it, so can I.*

> Nature does not hurry, yet everything is accomplished.
>
> —*Lao Tzu*

Mother Nature, we admire you.

> Freedom is nothing else but a chance to be better.
>
> —*Albert Camus*

I love a parade, big or small. Mardi Gras festivities are wildly awesome, but there's something so special about watching a Fourth of July parade in a small town. When we head to our little slice of heaven for the holiday, we like to pop the kids in strollers decorated with American flags and red, white, and blue beads and stars. Small groups of folks line up and march together down the street, waving and throwing candy. Hometown pride and pride in our country bust out everywhere, from banners hung on businesses to handmade signs along the route. Haley loves to see the fire trucks, and maybe next year Hope will spend time outside of the stroller marching in her own mini parade. I hope you get to share this important holiday with people you love. How grateful we are to everyone in the armed forces who protects our freedom to celebrate Independence Day in big and small ways. Thank you! We love you!

Don't let maturity kill your inner child.

Remember being a kid? When's the last time you had fun like one? I think we tend to shed that kind of silly way too soon in life. The other day, I was in a community playroom with Haley, and I asked her to join me in building a sandcastle. There was no sand, but we're good at pretending. As we were building, I played the Laurie Berkner song "The Goldfish." The music and lyrics sent us straight to our backs, and we became fish swimming in the ocean. I felt like a kid again, flailing my arms and legs without a care in the world! Other kids came over and joined us, and now we were a school of fishies in the sea. Laughing hysterically, I thought, *What's better than this right now?* If only we could act more free—like kids—more often. Swing on a swing, tickle your partner, run through a sprinkler. So much fun awaits, if we can just tap into our inner kid now and then and let loose!

Happiness cannot be traveled
to, owned, earned, worn,
or consumed.
Happiness is the spiritual
experience of living
every minute with love,
grace, and gratitude.

—DENIS WAITLEY

And how wonderful that those last three don't even cost a dime!

HK

I finally got eight hours of sleep. Took me four days, but whatever.

Exactly! And my Fitbit was *not* happy about my stats.

> Where you come from doesn't necessarily determine where you're going in life.

There's something so sweet about photos of little girls looking up at ballet dancer Misty Copeland, and when you listen to Misty talk, you know those kids' dreams are in good hands. At thirty-seven, Misty knows she's changing the face of ballet, as the first African American woman to be promoted to principal dancer in the history of the prestigious American Ballet Theatre. When I sat down with Misty, she said any assumption that she had a privileged upbringing is wrong. "Growing up in a single-parent home, one of six children, I was living in a hotel when I started dancing," she explained. That's why Misty loves the quote "Where you come from doesn't necessarily determine where you're going in life."

She said the personal struggles she faced as a child gave her the perseverance required to advance in the demanding world of ballet. Unique in her field, Misty encourages young people to be themselves and to tune out negativity, saying, "Don't let other people's words define you."

Never judge a book by its cover.

My best friend, Karen, chose this quote, unsure of its origins. "I'm not sure who said it first, but my mom has probably said it the most," Karen explained. "It's one of the best lessons she instilled in me from the earliest age, and I've tried to impart that message to my own daughter." Ever since I've known Karen, she's lived this way, always open to a connection with anyone, always searching for a way to include everyone. "How quick we are to judge based on what only the naked eye can see," Karen said. "The beauty lies within. Take the time to discover it."

I am too positive
to be doubtful,
too optimistic
to be fearful,
and
too determined
to be defeated.

Could this be you, too? Go get 'em!

> The only way to make sense out of change is to plunge into it, move with it, and join the dance. —*Alan Watts*

The change. I still have hot flashes due to menopause, but not as many as during the "heat" of the battle with my waning estrogen. In a *Today* segment, Dr. Lauren Streicher, a professor of obstetrics and gynecology at Northwestern University, explained that menopause means a woman's estrogen tank is on empty and the ovaries aren't going to kick back in. She broke the bad news that 80 percent of women get hot flashes that will last between five and ten years. The worst of it for me was sweating profusely on-air . . . out of nowhere. I briefly tried an herb called black cohosh, but mostly I drove Joel crazy with my yo-yo internal temperature. "Can we turn the heat down a bit?" he'd say, sweating. "Nope. We're freezing now." In case of a steamy night, I keep a fan on my nightstand. When I blast it, my face looks like I'm pulling three G's on a fighter jet, but whatever. We do what we have to do, right, ladies? Onward.

> There is a fountain of youth: it is your mind, your talents, the creativity you bring to your life and the lives of people you love. When you learn to tap this source, you will truly have defeated age.
>
> —*Sophia Loren*

But what about coconut oil? Jenna poked fun at me on our show when all of my "favorite things" kept including coconut as an ingredient. What can I say? I'm nuts for coconuts! Right now in my bathroom cabinet: Shea Moisture's Head-to-Toe Nourishing Hydration coconut oil, Daily Hydration Overnight Face Oil with coconut milk and acacia senegal, Daily Hydration Face Milk Cleanser with coconut milk, and Daily Hydration Face Lotion with coconut milk and acacia senegal, and RMS Beauty's the Ultimate Makeup Remover wipes with raw coconut oil.

Life takes you to unexpected places, love brings you home.

None of us expected to be quarantined at home for months because of a treacherous pandemic. Actress and restaurateur Ayesha Curry, who's married to NBA superstar Steph Curry, described their time in isolation with three young kids as "sweet chaos." When I spoke with her on *Today*, she joked that they had to order a basketball hoop to keep the kids busy. "Even basketball players don't want to bring their work home with them," she said. Ayesha has a magazine called *Sweet July*, because all good things happened for her in this month—her wedding and the births of all three of her children. In the latest edition, she listed five simple habits to adopt to maintain a sense of normalcy during unsettling times:

1. Make your bed
2. Get dressed
3. Plan meals and set a schedule
4. Get moving
5. Drink wine, eat bread

> In all this world there is nothing so beautiful as a happy child.
>
> —*L. Frank Baum*

One day I showed up half an hour early to pick up Haley from preschool. I'm so glad I did because something beautiful unfolded. Walking between buildings, the kids had formed a train and Haley was serving as the caboose. When she caught a glimpse of me, she looked surprised, and then a big smile lit up her face. As the train chugged by me, I heard her say with glee to a friend, "That's my mom!" She then broke off the train and ran to me, flinging herself into my arms. My heart exploded! What a sweet moment for us both. Haley ran back into line and kept pointing me out: "That's my mom! That's my mom!"

There are no goodbyes for us. Wherever you are, you will always be in my heart. —*Mahatma Gandhi*

This makes me think of a tiny photo tucked inside a gold locket.

Sometimes the person who tries to keep everyone happy is always the most lonely person.

There are peacemakers in every family—the people frantically sweeping eggshells out of the way so no one walks on them. Maybe they're lonely because they haven't carved out any time to connect with real life . . . warts and all.

> Kindness can become its own motive. We are made kind
> by being kind. —*Eric Hoffer*

It's never fun to embarrass ourselves, but most of us don't do it in front of our heroes. Jessica Simpson did, and she's forever grateful that Dolly Parton showed her mercy. When I interviewed Jessica the week she released her memoir, *Open Book*, I could see that the memory of that moment still stung. In 2006, Jessica was asked to perform "9 to 5" at the Kennedy Center Honors to pay tribute to her idol Dolly. Jessica was abusing alcohol during that time in her life, and because her then-boyfriend John Mayer had broken up with her earlier in the day, she drank before walking onstage before a packed house. Jessica started singing but couldn't connect with the audience or the song. "I froze," she said. "And then I just said I was sorry. And that Dolly deserved better." She left the stage, crushed and embarrassed. In her dressing room, a knock at the door revealed itself to be Dolly. "'Don't worry about it, honey,' she said. 'Even I've messed up before.'" From Dolly, a beautiful reminder to rescue each other whenever we can.

Saying "Hello," "Good morning," or a Kind Word will not cause brain damage.   —*Ty Howard*

Nor will saying thank you when someone opens the door for us!

We are made to persist;
that's how we find
out who we are.

—TOBIAS WOLFF

Imagine if a caterpillar stopped midway through her journey. She'd never take flight!

HK

July 20

This one is a bit of an "ouch," isn't it? An ugly truth we don't want pointed out. I think we can all relate to this concept . . . staying put in a situation, location, or relationship when we know it's time to move on. Change can be complicated and scary, so sometimes it's easier to just tough out the status quo. I've "shrunk" before to accommodate a relationship, and I learned the long and hard way that minimizing anything about yourself isn't healthy for either person. I think over-staying our welcome in areas of our life we've outgrown is simply a waste of precious time—time we could use to create our very best life. It's never fun to think, *I wish I had done this a long time ago.* Maybe today is the day you stop shrinking and start stretching. Take a deep breath, reach up over your head, and imagine where you really belong. Dear scared self—you've *got* this.

Me: Let me sleep.

Brain: LOL no, let's stay awake and remember every stupid decision you made in your life.

Me: Okay.

The worst!

To learn patience is not to rebel against every hardship.

—*Henri Nouwen*

I think this is a first cousin to having grace under pressure.

Self-care is giving the world the best of you, instead of what's left of you.   —*Katie Reed*

Sometimes my schedule—like yours—is particularly jam-packed. After a few days of long travel and short turnarounds, I was running on fumes. Staying awake at work was challenging, and I felt sick to my stomach. Determined to take care of myself, I made a plan: dinner for everybody at five o'clock; by six Hope will have a bottle in her mouth and Haley's bath will be running. Joel was traveling, so once the kids were down, that bed was my main focus. When I got home, it was boom boom boom. As Hope sucked on her bottle, her face said, *Isn't this early?* Yep, good night. I bathed Haley but didn't wash her hair. We read two books, and she tried to pull her stall tactic: "Gotta poop." Nope. I crawled into bed at seven fifteen (angels singing) with a box of Wheat Thins and played Candy Crush on my phone. I was *so* happy. By seven thirty, zzzzzz. It's so true: without rest, we're not our best!

Improvement
begins
with
I.

We see what you did there! It's up to us.

Never let a stumble in the road be the end of your journey.

Brush off the dirt and keep working toward that big finish!

True love stories never have endings.   —*Richard Bach*

We interviewed two friends on *Today* who happened upon old love letters and, ultimately, quite a story to tell. Lindsy Wolke and Megan Grant found the letters in a relics shop, and when they couldn't tear themselves away from reading a few, they bought all twenty-one. "The notes were just so beautifully written," said Megan. "Reading them just made your heart melt. It was like reading a book." When it became clear the letter writers were in love and separated by World War II, the friends wanted to find and meet "Ilaine" and "Elias." Unfortunately, both had died, but the women did contact one of their children, Barbara, who had no idea the letters existed. Not trusting the mail, the friends drove the missives eight hundred miles from Tennessee to Barbara, in New Jersey. "It's very heartwarming and is something we never expected," Barbara said, "but it's a treasure to have and be able to pass down to our children and grandchildren." So much to love here! What a beautiful gesture, Lindsy and Megan.

Your soul is attracted to people the same way flowers are attracted to the sun. Surround yourself only with those who want to see you grow.

A librarian in Lincoln, Nebraska, was determined to keep her 750 elementary students learning and growing during the COVID-19 crisis. Every single school day, Betsy Thomas used a green screen in her basement to record *Mrs. Thomas's Daily Storytime*. Wearing elaborate costumes ranging from a pirate to a forklift operator, she brought books alive for her young viewers. One video even featured her wearing pig ears reading a book to an actual piglet! Because my mom worked at the Library of Congress for thirty-five years, I have a special love for librarians and was so excited to join the school in a special surprise for their beloved librarian. While I distracted Betsy on a video phone call, her fully costumed students gathered on her front lawn. When she opened the front door, there were her kids! They waved and showed off their storybook character outfits. Moved to tears, Betsy said, "That's why all teachers do it, is because of the kids." We love you, Betsy, and all of our dedicated teachers everywhere!

One of the hardest decisions made in life is to choose which bridge to burn and which bridge to cross.

I don't like the idea of burning any bridges. Let's reframe this as "choosing which bridge to bid adieu and which bridge to cross."

> You are never too old to set another goal or to dream a
> new dream.   —*Les Brown*

Jenna surprised me on-air the week our live show *Hoda & Jenna &
Friends* debuted. She popped up off her seat to tell me that Oprah was
our guest on Friday! We'd tacked a photo of her on a vision board
we'd created for our new show . . . hoping . . . and now the Queen of
Daytime TV was booked! Turns out, Jenna did a bang-up job of
wooing O with a handwritten note, flowers, and a book. The girl's
got game! When our "O Countdown Clock" finally hit zero and
Oprah walked on set, the studio audience—and Jenna and I—went
wild. I couldn't hold back the tears, overwhelmed by decades of my
appreciation for the way Oprah holds someone's heart in her hand
with so much care. How cool is it that even in our midfifties we can
feel those first-day-of-school-Christmas-morning butterflies? Meeting Oprah reminded me of that. Thank you, Jenna, for such a meaningful surprise. And, Oprah? Please visit us anytime!

> Childhood means simplicity. Look at the world with the child's eye . . . it is very beautiful. —*Kailash Satyarthi*

To help with sleep management, Joel and I put a light fixture in Haley's bedroom to help her determine when it's time to get up. When the light turns green, the song "Twinkle, Twinkle, Little Star" plays. So cute! One morning, when Haley got the "go" sign, she called out for me. I walked in and there she was, cozied up in her pajamas on the bed. As the song played, she took my hands and said, "Mommy, let's dance." *Melt.* As we took a spin around her room, she noticed that I was tearing up a bit, overcome by such a sweet moment. Haley said, "Mommy, maybe we can do this every time you come in." That kid. Simply beautiful.

> I survived because the fire inside me burned brighter than
> the fire around me.   —*Joshua Graham, in* Fallout

Our burning love for one another during the COVID-19 crisis would not be denied. We found a variety of ways to safely express how much our friends and family meant to us. In the UK, a father had to distance himself from his six-year-old daughter, Carmela, because he delivered coronavirus samples to British labs for testing. The combination of his at-risk job and her muscular dystrophy required that he live in the backyard garden shed when he wasn't working. On *Today*, we aired a sweet video of their daddy-daughter daily routine. Using a series of hand signals, they took turns saying, "I love you this much." "I" was pointing to their eye, "love" was a hand over their heart, "you" was pointing at each other, and arms spread wide was "this much." The cherry on top was blowing kisses back and forth. Dad, we can only imagine how good it felt to finally hug your daughter. The "ask" was so painful during that time: stay away from the people you love to protect them.

> Life is a beautiful collection of temporary experiences. Treasure your unique collection, and enjoy sharing it with others.
> —*Matthew Kahn*

For nearly a decade, Maria Shriver has shared her weekly online newsletter, *Sunday Paper*. Her words never fail to inspire readers, including a woman named Sheri Lyons, who started what she calls the Sunday Paper Dinner Club. In a post, Maria had encouraged people to invite new faces to their dinner table, and the idea resonated with Sheri. "It all started with twelve people. People with different perspectives and different experiences," she said. "My husband would say, 'These people are fantastic. How do you know them?' And I'd say, 'I don't; I just met them.'" Her weekly dinner invitation on social media now draws people from twenty states and three countries, and dinner has moved to a Long Island recreational center to accommodate the crowd. To me, this just shows how many of us crave connection. Maybe this month, take Maria up on her idea and put out an extra plate or two on your dinner table. And if you're hungry for meaning and positivity, read *Sunday Paper*.

The tans will fade but the memories will last forever.

Joel, my daughters, and I all love the beach, so my heart went out to a New Jersey family who had to cancel their beach vacation during the pandemic. On *Today*, we ran video of the very creative solution Mom came up with to "make it all better." She captured the moment when her kids, dressed in bathing suits and swim goggles, stood outside the bathroom door. "Are you ready to go to the beach?" she asked. The kids jumped up and down and screamed, "YES!" When they busted into the bathroom and looked around, they yelled, "We're at the beach! Yeah!" Way to go, Mom! She'd filled the tub with water and snow saucers with sand, buckets, and shovels. Paper fish and palm trees were taped around the room. Cutout clouds and the sun completed the seaside scene. Mom said not only did the kids play at "the beach" for three hours, the "ocean" knocked out bath time, too!

> There is no path to happiness. Happiness is the path.
>
> —*A. J. Muste*

One of the happiest people I know is Joy Bauer, *Today*'s health and nutrition expert. Joy's a genius at creating nutritious recipes that also taste amazing. In her latest book, *Joy Bauer's Superfood!*, she offers "150 recipes for eternal youth." On the cover, Joy looks about sixteen, so they obviously work. Here's a recipe from her book that I thought you might enjoy:

LOADED BELL PEPPER NACHOS

Cut 6 red bell peppers into quartered "chips"; remove seeds

Sauté 1 pound ground meat; add a taco seasoning packet plus ⅔ cup water, ¾ cup both black beans and corn, ¼ cup jalapenos (optional)

Spoon above into pepper boats; sprinkle on 1 cup reduced-fat cheese

Bake on oiled baking sheet at 375 degrees F for about ten minutes

Add salsa, cilantro, sour cream (optional)

Nothing looks as good as healthy feels.

When *Today* producers asked Jenna and me to weigh ourselves on-air for a health segment, we immediately agreed. As moms, we want our kids to *not* have the same hang-ups with weight that we both did as heftier young women. Now, that's not to say either of us was happy with the numbers when we stepped on the scale. The next step was our trying the trendy "intermittent fasting" method to lose weight and boost our brain health and energy. Because I get up at three a.m., the concept of waiting to eat until ten in the morning (along with no food after six p.m.) seemed daunting. But Jenna and I agreed to fast intermittently for one month. How did it go? I gotta say, even after one day I felt more alert than usual. I managed to make it through the month, but we'll see by the time you read this whether I've kept it up. (There's a good chance I may once again be shoveling Pirate's Booty into my mouth before bed.)

Behind every young child who believes in himself is a parent who believed first. —*Matthew L. Jacobson*

Sometimes children seem to have a way of seeing things more clearly. That's why I spoke to a group of young people during the Black Lives Matter movement in June 2020. I asked a small group of kids what they thought would help fix the problem of people treating others unfairly. A fifteen-year-old girl named Marley Dias really blew me away with her positive energy. She'd already campaigned to get thousands of books about black girls into schools! "The moment we're living in is kind of frustrating because it feels as though it's an attack on people that look like me," she said. "I think people need to understand that racism exists, and that we need to understand that it's okay to be black, it's okay to be white, it's okay to be Pacific Islander, and it's all these differences that in fact make this country beautiful and amazing and that makes us the people that we are." I felt better about the future having heard the kids agree on this one simple thought: we're all the same.

> Your mind is your instrument. —*Remez Sasson*

It's an ongoing challenge, so we have to tune our "instrument" from time to time. Today seems like a good day to adjust the pitch of our thoughts.

1. Positive
2. Encouraging
3. Hopeful
4. Grateful
5. Determined
6. Caring

You've got to stay strong to be strong in tough times.

—*Tilman J. Fertitta*

In 2019, I hired trainer Will Weber. I was fifty-five years old with two small children. Because I want to play with my kids for many years to come, I needed help. "So, do you want cut arms? Toned abs?" Will asked me. I told him no. What I wanted was to be able to get up and down off the floor one hundred times a day. I wanted to be able to throw my thirty-five-pound daughter up in the air and catch her. I've always dragged myself to the gym to stay healthy, but I was never the person who loved it. Now, with two little reasons to get and stay strong, my trips to the gym have more meaning. As my girls grow, Will keeps increasing the weights. I want to be able to walk around holding both daughters, should I need to. Don't get me wrong, working out still hurts, but something's different—it hurts so good.

You are successful the moment you start moving toward a worthwhile goal.

—CHARLES CARLSON

I like that. The very first step we take is *already* a win.

Of all the paths you take in life, make sure a few of them are dirt.

For me, that quote would end with the word "sand," but the meaning remains the same: get outside!

If you suddenly feel joy, don't hesitate. Give in.

—*Mary Oliver*

I think children do this best, which is one reason I'm so drawn to them. You can't miss a kid experiencing joy—the giggling and jumping up and down is unmistakable! Kids give in to joy freely and frequently, sometimes because of something as simple as a cardboard box that for whatever reason is *awesome*. Maybe adults feel like they can't afford to linger long in joy, beholden to deadlines and responsibilities. If you're lucky enough to feel joyful today—and I hope you are—try not to rush it.

Know that you are the perfect age. Each year is special and precious, for you shall only live it once. Be comfortable with growing older.

—*Louise L. Hay*

I have a mostly healthy relationship with aging. My only angst with being in my fifties is that my daughters are very young. I suppose it makes every day with these little angels that much sweeter.

> I dwell in Possibility.
>
> *—Emily Dickinson*

This just busts the door wide open to potential, doesn't it? To linger as best and often as we can in optimism isn't just healthy, it's an action plan. If our mind's eye sees each opportunity as possible, we're on our way to probable! If you can today, consider, *Why not me?*

> The beauty of the written word is that it can be held close to the heart and read over and over again.
>
> —*Florence Littauer*

Do you write love letters? Most of us don't write letters of any kind anymore. That's why I was so moved listening to Jenna share a note written by her grandfather George H. W. Bush. He wrote the letter to Barbara Bush on their anniversary: "Will you marry me? Oops, I forgot. You did that forty-nine years ago today! I was very happy on that day in 1945, but I am even happier today. You've given me joy few men know. I've climbed perhaps the highest mountain in the world, but even that cannot hold a candle to being Barbara's husband." I mean, just beautiful. The couple spent more than sixty years writing love letters to each other. Barbara's were lost when George's plane was shot down during World War II, but his live on: "I love you precious with all my heart, and to know that you love me means my life."

You cannot rise without understanding what you're rising from.

Whenever I've gone through a difficult chapter—from divorce to breast cancer—it's the positive lessons that have served as rungs of a ladder . . . once I'm ready to look for them. Journaling about what I've learned has helped me to climb up and out—to rejoin life armed with all the good stuff that arose from a bad experience.

HK

Me as a lawyer: Okay, well first of all, that was rude.

Ha! My great-aunt Mufidah was the first female lawyer in Egypt, a true pioneer. My mom's mother's sister was also the first married woman to enroll at Cairo University's Faculty of Law and the first mother to graduate from the institution, raising a total of nine children. Initially compensated for her services in eggs and fruit, my intrepid great-aunt went on to plead more than four hundred cases. Mufidah was also a strong proponent of women, cofounding the National Feminist Party, which fought for and ultimately won women's right to vote in Egypt. I have fond memories of my great-aunt, whom we always visited during family trips abroad. When I was working in New Orleans, I flew to Egypt to interview Mufidah. Boy, walking around the courthouse with her was like having Tina Turner on my arm. She was a legal rock star! A priceless story she shared with me was of a fellow lawyer's telling her to get him a cup of tea. Her answer: "I'm not getting your tea. I'm a lawyer just like you."

> How old would you be if you didn't know how old you are?
> —*Satchel Paige*

The name of her book says it all: *Why Did I Come into This Room?* Journalist Joan Lunden nailed the title for her book about aging, which she released when she was sixty-nine. Sitting across from her as she shared her experience with growing older, I noted how vibrant she looked, even as she was raising two sets of teenage twins and three older children! I've always admired Joan and the way she's handled herself with grace and grit throughout her career and in her personal life. As we chatted, Joan shared her mom's advice to make plans throughout our lives. "She said, 'Half the fun about doing anything is anticipating it,' and never is that more true than in this pivotal point in our fifties and sixties." Joan offers these additional tips on "declining to decline":

- Get some sunshine and fresh air
- Put more energy into your voice
- Do a good deed
- Act happy
- Watch a funny TV show or movie

> Be a part of something bigger than yourself.

I wasn't familiar with Professor Ibram X. Kendi before I read his book *Stamped from the Beginning*. He's a *New York Times* bestselling author, the Andrew Mellon Professor of the Humanities and the founding director of the Boston University Center for Antiracist Research. When Brené Brown interviewed him on her podcast about his book *How to Be an Antiracist*, he talked about being both horrified and energized at such an important time in history, when a man's death was uniting people against the scourge of racism. His perspective on being black in America included the reality of feeling a disproportionate amount of danger from repression, violence, and disease, like COVID-19. His goal is to help people identify and oppose racism, and to see ourselves and each other as human beings. "The heartbeat historically of racism has been denial," Ibram said. "By contrast the heartbeat of antiracism is confession, is admission, is acknowledgment, is the willingness to be vulnerable." He added that we can't solve a problem with ourselves or our country if we don't admit there is one.

> Never be in a hurry; do everything quietly and in a calm
> spirit. Do not lose your inner peace for anything whatso-
> ever, even if your whole world seems upset.
>
> —*Saint Francis de Sales*

Having children has made my life busier but, even more so, has slowed me down. Hanging out with my two daughters forces me to focus solely on them, freeing me from the chaos that often blows up on my phone. Having our little family provides me an immense amount of inner peace, because being a mom is what I'm supposed to be doing. I'm a work in progress when it comes to *not* being a tornado of activity, but I'm trying to do better. I don't want to hurry anything when it comes to Haley and Hope.

> Some people believe holding on and hanging in there are signs of great strength. However, there are times when it takes much more strength to know when to let go and then do it.
>
> —*Ann Landers*

One day, my *Today* colleague Sheinelle Jones walked into the makeup room looking burdened. She slunk into a chair, upset that she was only spending time with her three young kids on Sundays because she worked the other six days. "Why do you work Saturdays?" Maria Shriver asked. "Well, it's my show." Maria nodded. "But do you *want* to do it?" Sheinelle said, "If I don't, someone else will." Maria then shared her story of an NBC boss's response when she expressed burnout from working double shifts. He said, "I'll have that position filled before you hit L for lobby in the elevator." Within several months, Sheinelle announced her departure from the weekend show. When I next saw her I said, "Hey, Sheinelle—you work five days a week." She smiled and started doing a little dance in the studio! I guess sometimes we have to let go of *our thing* if it's standing in the way of something even more valuable—in Sheinelle's case, Uche, Clara, and Kayin.

The greatest legacy we can leave our children is happy memories.

—OG MANDINO

I believe this is easier than we think, too. Happy childhood memories usually involve something so simple: a bicycle, a swing set, a campfire, a diving board, a picnic.

HK

The most confused we ever get is when we try to convince our heads of something our hearts know is a lie.

The struggle is real.

> You do not have to make your children into wonderful people. You just have to remind them that they are wonderful people. If you do this consistently from the day they are born, they will believe it easily. —*William Martin*

I was so moved by what award-winning actor Sterling K. Brown told Willie Geist about his career and personal life. When the topic of loss came up during the interview, Sterling said his father had a heart attack when he was only ten and his father was forty-five. He shared a vivid memory of paramedics wheeling his father out of the house, the last time he saw him alive. "As they're carrying him out on the stretcher, he looks at me over the railing and he winks. . . . He filled me up with so much love, and so while the time was short, it was everything that I could have hoped for for ten years." Sterling says he's using his father's example to raise his two sons, eight and four years old. What a beautiful reminder—to love each other as hard as we can for as long as we're together.

Look for something positive in each day, even if some days you have to look a little harder. Let the challenges make you strong.

Sometimes looking for the positive means running interference on the negative. That's what one single mom did during the coronavirus crisis. At a time when we were advised to stay home as much as possible, that was nearly *im*possible for parents without a partner or day care for their kids, who were home from school. A Texas mom knew she'd get dirty looks and nasty comments in the grocery store because her daughter would be with her, so she did her best to avoid the negativity. Before putting little BellaRose in the shopping cart, MaryAnne Resendez popped a mask on her and taped this sign to her back:

I am only 5. I can't stay home alone so I have to buy groceries with my Mommy . . . Before you start judging, stay back 6 feet.

MaryAnne was happy to share on Facebook that her sign worked, which encouraged other stressed parents to follow her lead.

Success happens when we're
not in the mood to make
a healthy choice, but
we do anyway.

Okay, right . . . but sometimes we have to scarf down cinnamon coffee cake with crumbly topping. It happens.

HK

> Learn to light a candle in the darkest moments of some-
> one's life. Be the light that helps others see; it is what gives
> life its deepest significance. —*Roy T. Bennett*

Our country wanted to understand, to finally have conversations about race and racism in America following the police-officer-caused death of George Floyd. I spoke with two mothers who, tragically, had also lost sons at the hands of police. In 2014, Gwen Carr's forty-three-year-old son, Eric Garner, died from a New York City police officer's illegal chokehold. She said she's constantly concerned for her remaining children. "When they go out, if I hear any noise outside, here I go running to the window, because you don't know who's going to come up and say your child is dead, your child's been shot. So this is what we go through as black mothers in America." Se'Quette Clark's son Stephon Clark was twenty-three when he was shot in his grandmother's backyard in 2018, after police officers mistook his cell phone for a gun. She calls the arrests and firings of officers involved with George Floyd justice: "It's saying that our lives and the lives of our children matter. . . . I thank God that change is coming."

> You don't need everyone to love you, just a few good people.
>
> —*Charity Barnum, in* The Greatest Showman

Apparently, Mrs. B said this to her famous husband, P. T. Barnum, during the 1800s. Many decades later, these words resonate even more as we all navigate social media.

There are no seven wonders
of the world in the eyes of a child.
There are seven million.

—WALT STREIGHTIFF

I witnessed this on Easter when I gave Haley an Easter basket filled with goodies. She went straight for an extra-large pink rubber ball. Her eyes wide, she picked up the ball and asked, "What is this?" She then bounced it and giggled. Oh my. To learn for the first time what a big round bouncy thing is . . . truly a wonder.

HK

> Other things may change us, but we start and end with the family.
>
> —*Anthony Brandt*

Rainy days can definitely be cozy—a great time to hunker down with a good book or movie. Several gloomies in a row, though, can make you and your kids stir-crazy. That was the case on a gray, wet afternoon in New York City. Sheets of rain beat against the windows as my girls busied themselves with snacks and toys, until even those pleasures failed to entertain. That's when I turned to music for a rescue. "Alexa, play 'Rainy Day People,'" I said. When Gordon Lightfoot's soothing voice filled the air, I sang along to Haley and Hope. Joel wandered downstairs and took me into his arms for a slow dance. Haley started giggling, both hands covering her mouth. Hope looked on, curious. About halfway through the song, Haley walked over and wrapped her arms around our legs, swaying along to the music. She then looked up and said, "We're family." I couldn't believe it! *So* beautiful . . . my favorite minute of that day—maybe even of the month. Oh, how I love my rainy-day people.

Good friends are like stars; you don't always see them but you know they are there.

A beautiful video that went viral in 2017 surged in views again during the COVID-19 pandemic after it was posted on Twitter. It's an uplifting must-see for any and all times! A Seattle dad and his four-year-old daughter are seen sitting on the couch singing the Randy Newman song "You've Got a Friend in Me." They take turns singing verses, Josh Crosby playing the guitar and little Claire fiddling with her braided ponytail throughout. Adorable! Both have great pipes, and when we interviewed Josh on *Today,* he said, "I think that people are realizing that family time and friends are a bright light in the midst of all this tragedy. We're sticking together through something scary and it's pretty awesome." Pretty awesome indeed, Crosby family. If you need a one-two punch of positivity, search the internet for Josh and Claire's tender duet.

> What brings us to tears, will lead us to grace. Our pain is never wasted.
> —*Bob Goff*

A talented cook herself, Natalie Morales was the perfect person to interview actress and author Tembi Locke about her memoir *From Scratch: A Memoir of Love, Sicily, and Finding Home*. They spoke in Tembi's kitchen about how she navigated losing the love of her life, Sicilian chef Saro Gullo. In 2002, the couple was devastated by his cancer diagnosis, resulting in a ten-year battle with the disease. Their journey was difficult but also included a bright spot—the adoption of their daughter, Zoela. "I think one of the things I learned: life is still happening all around us, and for us," she said. "We'd always wanted to be parents, and this felt like the perfect path." When Saro died in 2012, Tembi began to cook to feel closer to him, resulting in the book's recipes. Tembi told Natalie that over time, she's discovered the blessings that arose from Saro's illness. "It deepened our marriage, and our friendship became deeper and greater, because we got to see parts of each other that we might not have been asked to step forward." Grace.

> Quiet the mind, and the soul will speak.
>
> —*Ma Jaya Sati Bhagavati*

On *Today*, I interviewed Jay Shetty, a purpose coach, about relieving stress and anxiety. A former monk, Jay sang the praises of solitude and its remarkable power of renewal. He recommended finding one thing to do alone each day that makes you happy, like learning something new or cracking a book. Jay also suggested moments of creativity—like painting—or whatever fills you up, even for a few minutes. He encouraged creating an environment filled with joyful sights and sounds—framed photos, your kids' drawings, your favorite music. Smells, too, can be mood changers. Jay suggests lighting a candle or cooking your favorite dish. I believe in all of those tips and actually do most of them. I also find it soothing to start and end my day with something positive. I keep something to read on my nightstand so I nourish myself in the morning and at night—the bookends of each day. In this busy life, on this very day, may you find a way to give your soul a chance to speak.

> The best way to cheer yourself is to try to cheer someone else up. —*Mark Twain*

Our souls were soothed by doing something kind for others during the pandemic. So much in our daily lives felt out of control, but helping someone was well within reach. *Today* covered countless stories of Americans' having each other's backs, including coworkers at a Washington State Trader Joe's. Matthew Simmons, a deaf employee, said that the use of protective masks made it very difficult for him to assist customers, whose lips were covered. "Some of the times, customers didn't want to lower down their masks and shook their heads 'no' and walked away from me," Matthew explained. "It made me upset because I couldn't help." When Matthew shared his frustration with colleagues, several teamed up to solve the problem. They armed Matthew with small whiteboards so everyone could safely communicate and customized his work shirt with "I read lips" on the front, and "Please tap me on the shoulder for help" on the back. A win for everyone! And boy, did our weary grocery store workers need a boost during those very stressful months.

The future is always beginning now. —*Mark Strand*

The future just stamped "CONFIRMED" on this one!

> Unity is strength. When there is teamwork and collaboration, wonderful things can be achieved.
>
> —*Mattie Stepanek*

During the coronavirus crisis, people across the world were physically divided for weeks on end in an effort to stop the spread. Before long, we all yearned to be reunited with the people we loved and as a healthy country. You may recall the countless images of people using windowpanes to touch palms, meet newborns, and share a dance or news of an engagement, all both heartbreaking and heartwarming. On *Today*, we loved the uplifting story of a Maryland mom who came up with a great idea for her own family that ended up uniting the neighborhood. Because her young daughters were home from school, Mom wanted them to have a familiar routine each morning. So, carrying an American flag, the trio walked out to the driveway and recited the Pledge of Allegiance, just like the little girls did in school. Neighbors noticed and joined in! The morning pledge became a way for folks to check on each other and to reunite safely, if only for a few minutes. Way to go, Mom. Unity *is* strength.

Silence is golden . . . unless you have kids, then . . . silence is just suspicious.

Honey? Honey?! [Child's first and middle name here!]

It's during the worst storms
of your life that you will
get to see the true colors
of the people who
say they care for you.

Experiencing the pandemic with Joel further solidified that I've made the right choice in a partner for life. He was rock-solid, calm, logical, and helpful, and when he said that everything was going to be okay, I believed him.

HK

> Anxiety happens when you think you have to figure out everything all at once. Breathe. You're strong. You got this. Take it day by day. —*Karen Salmansohn*

I find it hard to slow down, often sprinting from point A to point Z and back. But one evening, as I was putting the kids down for the night, Haley reminded me that I needed to downshift. "Read slower, Mommy," she said. As Hope slept beside us in bed, I was hurrying through a book with Haley. Joel and I were going to the Zac Brown concert and all I could hear in my head was *ticktock*. "Read softer, Mommy, Hope is sleeping," Haley whispered. She kept pulling me back into the moment, where I should have been. When it was time for her to brush her teeth, I skipped putting on my sunglasses like I normally do, signaling that her teeth were so white I had to wear shades. "Mommy, you didn't put the glasses on." Gosh, all those little rituals mattered to Haley, and I was rushing through the good stuff. I think sometimes it's our kids who remind us to tap the brakes . . . just like the Zac Brown song "No Hurry."

> Sometimes the greatest thing to come out of all your hard work isn't what you get for it, but what you become for it.
>
> —*Steve Maraboli*

Jenna and I were chatting with Andy Cohen on his show, *Watch What Happens Live*, when a caller asked an interesting question. She wanted to know what the biggest misconception is about being a first daughter. Jenna said it's hard to know what people truly think of you as a president's daughter, and that because she and her twin sister, Barbara, were in college during President Bush's terms, people often don't realize they didn't live in the White House. Jenna added, "Maybe people think that I'm not a hard worker, but I try to fight against that a little." I can tell you that without a doubt, Jenna *is* a hard worker. Not only is she busy at home raising three kids, she's a dedicated *Today* colleague, always willing to go the extra mile. Get this—in the first two weeks of our live show together, Jenna booked Oprah, Dolly Parton, and Michelle Obama! Way to kill it right out of the gate, Jenna. I love you.

> Live simply, love generously, care deeply, speak kindly, leave the rest to God. —*Ronald Reagan*

This is my best friend, Karen, so full of love and centered by faith. One day, she shared a beautiful image with me that I still think about. She said that a physician friend told her that whenever she feels down, she visualizes a large pair of hands, held open like a cozy nest. Then she imagines crawling up into the soft palms, where she curls up and feels protected.

> Between stimulus and response there is a space. In that space is our power to choose our response.

My "Quoted By" segment took on a bit more meaning during the coronavirus crisis, as we were all eager for inspiration. When I asked actress Rita Wilson for a quote that was close to her heart, she offered the above words. I can see why. She and her husband, Tom Hanks, were the first celebrities to report being diagnosed with the virus. Thankfully, both recovered. Rita said her journey through breast cancer helped dull the shock; she'd already realized that serious illness can befall anyone. Rita said it's important to take a pause during challenging times. "If you are in that state of feeling like, *Ahh!*—like you're just going to explode—remember that there is a space, and in that space you can choose how to react." Easier said than done, of course, but there was something so soothing about Rita's voice. "We are resilient as a people, and as Americans, and as human beings," she said. "We are going to get through this. We are going to be okay."

> Music washes away from the soul the dust of everyday life.
> —*Berthold Auerbach*

When we all holed up during the coronavirus crisis, so many of us relied on the internet for some daily social interaction. One of my favorite ways the web brought us together was through virtual concerts. If you missed "It Is Well with My Soul" sung by Nashville backup singers, look it up. Amazing! During such a joyless time, symphonies and philharmonics around the globe chose Beethoven's "Ode to Joy" to share with people stuck at home, desperate for comfort. What made the performances so unique was that each person was cozied up in their home, dressed in casual clothes, sharing their gift. In each little square on the screen you saw a person, isolated but connected through a common bond—the music. Because of the creativity and strength of the human spirit, music found its way into our homes and hearts during such a trying time. As always, thank you, music!

September 11

> A single sunbeam is enough to drive away many shadows.
>
> —*Saint Francis of Assisi*

This makes me think of the awesome power that a small act of kindness wields. One morning, my friend and driver Eddie surprised me with—literally— a very sweet gesture. The day before, as we were en route to work, I had been going on and on about my favorite junk food. When I got in the car the next morning, Eddie had packed the seat with Entenmann's cupcakes, cinnamon buns, and Devil Dogs. So Eddie! He always says, "You have to make adventures," and he sure did for me that morning. There's just something about the brightness of Eddie's spirit that draws you in; you want to soak up more of his light. He was the first person to meet baby Hope after Joel and I picked her up because he drove the three of us home. I made sure he was included in the Zoom call for her first birthday. Eddie will be there for our next milestone, too. See you at the wedding, Eddie!

Love is the greatest gift that one generation can leave to another.

—RICHARD GARNETT

Today is Grandparents Day, and in our house we'd call it Teta Day. Right now, in my mind, I see my mom snuggled up on the couch with Hope and Haley, under a blanket, watching the umpteenth episode of *Sesame Street*. That would be the best and only way my mom would want to celebrate Teta Day.

> Today is a brand-new day—a perfectly good reason to get
> up and start over. Never give up.   —*Richelle E. Goodrich*

Don't you just love a clean slate? Off you go, superstar!

Beauty is not in the face; beauty is a light in the heart.

—*Kahlil Gibran*

This is one of the many reasons I love watching *The Voice*. Chairs turn because the coaches are using their ears, not their eyes. They listen for a light in the heart.

The day you plant the seed is not the day you eat the fruit.

With a creative way to say, "Be patient." It's also a good reminder to get started! Can you plant the seed of something special today?

> Emotions are the language of the soul.

World-renowned speaker and author Brené Brown is the best at connecting and comforting people. During the COVID-19 crisis, I thought she offered good advice that worked not only in those dark times but throughout life's challenges. "Emotions can only really take you down when you're unaware of them," she said. "If you understand and can name them, you can walk through them." *I'm anxious, I'm disappointed, I feel afraid.* Brené suggested checking in with loved ones, including young kids. What and how are you feeling? Brené said her family created a set of rules to follow when their collective physical and mental energy isn't 100 percent:

No harsh words
No nice words with harsh faces
Say you're sorry
Accept apologies with thank-yous
More puns and knock-knock jokes

I hope you're 100 percent today, but if you're not, perhaps give a voice to whatever is burdening you.

> The great enemy of communication is the illusion of it.
>
> —*William Whyte*

So true! So many times we think we've gotten our point across to someone, but nothing changes. We wonder: was it a misfire by the messenger or the listener? Joel and I sometimes have to reboot—as do all couples—when we're not having enough meaningful conversations. You know when you find yourselves only talking about the weather or the kids or what's for dinner? That's when it's time to carve out some space for a sit-down—no kids, no phones, no small talk. (But not after eight p.m., please, because I'm running on fumes.)

> I'm not really a control freak, but . . . can I show you the right way to do that?

Ha! I don't know about your family, but in mine the control freaks were clearly revealed during Zoom sessions.

On Easter 2020, when we had to be apart because of the pandemic, our family's phones and tablet screens were chopped into four squares.

Me: Hala, stop and let Mom talk!
My mom: How do I turn on the Zoom?
Hala: I can't see Mom! Someone help Mom!
Adel: [calm silence]
Me: Just push the button, Mom!

Poor Joel had a front-row seat to our family's insanity as technology connected *and* revealed us. Well, revealed Hala and me . . .

The smallest act of kindness is worth more than the grandest intention.

So many small acts of kindness helped soothe us during the COVID-19 pandemic. I found myself bursting into tears watching or reading about some of them, and giggling at others, as we all tried to manage the whiplash of emotions from one minute to the next. Willie Geist, on his show *Sunday Today*, shared two stories in the segment "Sunday Mail."

Roberta from Pennsylvania wrote in to share a note that her school custodian left for her during the shutdown: *Roberta, I took your ivy plant home with me. I'll bring it back. Take care, Don C.* Heather from Texas, a second-grade schoolteacher, wrote to share that a student left flowers on her doorstep along with this note: *Mis. A.—I miss you. I miss science. My mom sucks as a teacher. Enjoy your flower. Love, Emerson.*

So dear, so funny . . . and that's how it rolled, day after day.

A good life is a collection of happy memories.

—Denis Waitley

Seems like a good day to make some!

Breathe. It's just a bad day, not a bad life.

Bad days can do that—make us feel like our life is *the worst*. But I find that a good night's sleep and writing down three things I'm grateful for helps put things into perspective. Hope today's a good one for you!

If you don't like the road you're walking, start paving another one!
—*Dolly Parton*

During a network interview, Dolly Parton was asked if she planned to retire. Her answer was classic Dolly! At seventy-three, Dolly said not only is she never retiring, she hopes to return to the cover of *Playboy* magazine at seventy-five. What a firecracker! When Jenna and I interviewed her on our show, her fifty-fourth wedding anniversary was approaching. So, Jenna asked Dolly about marriage advice for Joel and me, especially as everyone was isolating due to the COVID-19 pandemic. "I would say if you're trapped in the house with him, you might want to be in separate rooms," she joked. "The reason it worked for me is because I've stayed gone. I can't get away now. . . . I might find out who he is. We may not make it until the next anniversary." Ha! She said that laughter has been a constant in her marriage, and I think that's important, too. Your hubby's a lucky guy, Dolly, and so are we. You're a national treasure!

A simple smile. That's the start of opening your heart and being compassionate to others.

—*The Fourteenth Dalai Lama*

Billion-dollar idea:

A smoke alarm that shuts off when you yell, "I'M JUST COOKING!"

Yep! When the kitchen smells like burnt salmon.

I used to believe that prayer changes things,
but now I know that prayer changes us
and we change things.

—SAINT TERESA OF CALCUTTA

Maybe "the power of prayer" means—in part—that praying helps
give us the power to be and do better.

I hope the guy who invented autocorrect burns in hello.

Here are some funny actual autocorrect fails:

Boy: Can't wait to see you babe.

Girl: It's Friday. I'm getting pregnant tonight!

Boy: Shouldn't we talk first?

Girl: Oh my God! I wrote pringles and it autocorrected to pregnant.

Boy: I almost had a heart attack!

Boy 1: How was the date?

Boy 2: Not quite. First date we went to dinner and then I killed her in the woods outside her house and left.

Boy 1: Killing her seems a bit harsh.

Boy 2: KISSED, wtf.

Behind you, all your memories.

Before you, all your dreams.

Around you, all who love you.

Within you, all you need.

Those words stack up like a lovely cake, positivity baked into every layer.

> At the end of the day, a loving family should find everything forgivable.   —*Mark V. Olsen*

It's not easy for some people to say, "I'm sorry." We've all had a falling-out with a friend or family member, and it's such a yucky feeling having to worry about the awkward moment when you'll see them again. Maria's daughter Katherine Schwarzenegger Pratt wrote an informative how-to book called *The Gift of Forgiveness: Inspiring Stories from Those Who Have Overcome the Unforgivable.* When I spoke with her, Katherine explained that she interviewed twenty-two people who found peace by letting go of resentment. She said it was her own struggle with forgiveness that sparked the idea for this topic. "When I decided to write this book, I thought I had practiced forgiveness already," she said, "and so during the process of writing this book and interviewing these amazing people about their experiences, I realized I actually needed to go back and do more work." Katherine said, "Forgiveness takes time, but you can get there by hearing other people's stories." The reward, she says, is a feeling of freedom, of a weight being lifted. Relief, right? Maybe today's a good day to try . . .

> Be patient and tough; someday this pain will be useful to you.
>
> —*Ovid*

The relationship between Goldie Hawn and Kate Hudson is so dear. You can tell that the mother and daughter are also best friends. I love when either one of them joins us on the set of *Today*, because the energy level skyrockets and all bets are off about where the conversation will lead. That's why I was surprised to read in *People* magazine that Goldie changed baby Kate's name at the last minute, but I *wasn't* surprised by how direct she was about why. "She kicked me so hard in my vagina that I changed her name right on the spot," she said, "because she was tough." Classic Goldie! "I had named her Rebecca, and on the 405, I went, 'This is a Kate.'"

It's all connected. Your gifts, your circumstances, your purpose, your imperfections, your journey, your destiny. It's molding you. Embrace it.

I think the message here is, "Relax." But I think it's human nature to second-guess ourselves and our circumstances. Am I a good parent? Are my relationships solid? Can this job sustain me? What am I supposed to be doing? It's hard to just stop self-analyzing and live each day with faith that our journey is unfolding as it should. Plus, some yucky days aren't easy to embrace, right? Well, even if we can't refrain completely from questioning, maybe we can dial it back a bit. Today, let's just try to embrace life, which has a pretty good track record of having our best interests in mind . . . over time.

Do not judge others by your own standards, for everyone is making their way home, in the way they know best.

—*Leon Brown*

Craig Melvin's wife, Lindsay, sat down with his mother to talk about her experience as an African American growing up in South Carolina in the 1960s. Lindsay is white and wanted to know what she could learn from Betty Jo, how she could grow as a person and a parent to two biracial children. Mrs. Melvin shared memories of being spit on by children riding the bus as she walked to school, and using hand-me-down desks and books from the white schools. Bathrooms were segregated and the KKK was active within her community. Now sixty-five years old, Mrs. Melvin said that she knew her kids would not be given equal opportunity. "As the mother of black men and black grandboys, this world is a little bit different for them. . . . They have to compete a little bit harder. . . . So you teach your children from when they're younger that, 'I need you to be more.' You have to push them harder." When Lindsay asked Mrs. Melvin what she thought black Americans needed during such unsettling times, she said respect. "Respect how we are feeling."

Always trust your gut. It knows what your head hasn't figured out yet.

Gut check!

Broken crayons still color.

We all have a way to brighten the world, even if life has broken our spirit a bit.

It's like kids can just smell us relaxing.

. . . and then they pounce.

When we throw out the physical clutter, we clear our minds. When we throw out the mental clutter, we clear our souls.

—*Gail Blanke*

It's much easier for me to tackle mental messes. Actual clutter? Not so much. I swear I once had kitchen countertops . . .

The three *C*'s in life:
Choice, Chance, Change.

You must make a choice to take a chance or your life will never change.

The third *C* is the charm!

HK

If you don't ask, the answer is always no.   —*Nora Roberts*

Haley likes to ask other kids if they want to hold hands. I've been in the community playroom many times when she does. "Hold hands?" she'll say, her little hand held out as an offering. Sometimes the child will say no, and Haley will look back at me. "Okay, keep going," I'll tell her. Haley then walks to someone else and tries again. The scenario repeats itself and without fail, by the end of the play session, she's holding hands with someone. The lesson for me is, keep asking! If there's something you need or want, ask. And ask again if you get a no. As adults, we tend to read no as a rejection. Haley takes it as an opportunity to try again, and she's the one holding someone's hand at the end of the day. It's like the not-so-popular guy in high school dancing with someone. Maybe ten girls said no, but he's the one dancing and having fun because the eleventh said yes. If you get a no today, ask again.

Loving yourself isn't vanity, it is sanity.   —*Katrina Mayer*

When our self-worth is strong, haters sound like "blah blah blah."

> Courage, above all things, is the first quality of a warrior.
>
> —*Carl von Clausewitz*

During the time I was hosting a television show called *Your Total Health,* I was diagnosed with breast cancer. I remember my emotions were so raw, I was having trouble reading the script for a story about cancer and required several takes to get through it. That's why I so admired my colleague, correspondent Kristen Dahlgren, on the *Today* set one day. On her forty-seventh birthday, Kristen noticed a small dent in her breast, which turned out to be stage 2 cancer. She endured chemotherapy, hair loss, the whole nine yards. Still, just two months after her diagnosis, Kristen covered a story about St. Jude Children's Research Hospital and the medical breakthroughs made there. Surely thinking of her own daughter, Kristen bravely interviewed kids battling cancer. On set, as her taped story was airing, I said, "I can't believe you were able to cover that story . . . with all you're going through." Without skipping a beat, she said, "I cannot imagine what has happened to me is happening to children." I'm delighted to report that on April 29, 2020, Kristen tweeted this amazing update: *#CANCER FREE!*

> When you are kind to others, it not only changes you, it changes the world. —*Harold Kushner*

So many people found creative ways during the coronavirus quarantine to show their love for one another from afar. A little boy in Australia was captured in a viral video (credited to Anna Schonfeldt) finding a special delivery from Grandma in his family's mailbox.

Mom: What does it say?
Remy: Let's open it and see.
Mom: It says, "Remy. Love, Grandma."
Remy works his little fingers hard to open a small white bag.
Remy: Is it a doughnut? Is it a doughnut?
With pure glee, Remy pulls out a chocolate-covered doughnut!
   Before taking a big bite, he does a little dance.
Remy: It's a dooooooooughnut!

Way to go, Grandma! Your sweet gesture made us want to do a happy dance, too.

> Cry. Forgive. Learn. Move on. Let your tears water the seeds of your future happiness. —*Steve Maraboli*

I love my colleague Dylan and her husband, Brian Fichera. When they shared with me that Brian had contracted the coronavirus, I was so scared for them. Dylan had given birth to Ollie months earlier, and little Calvin was just three years old. Immediately, Brian quarantined himself in Calvin's room, joking later about the cramped quarters: "Our neighbors saw a grown man getting out of a bunk bed every day." Dylan held down the fort as she worried for her very sick husband. Brian described the experience as hairy, scary, and serious, sharing his thoughts on Instagram:

The headaches were debilitating. No amount of Tylenol could put a dent in my headaches or temperature. There was also an emotional component to this disease. I cried. ALOT. It feels like you're snorkeling through a cocktail straw.

Brian, thank God, recovered and the family stayed safe. Tears of joy could now water the seeds of their future happiness.

A good teacher is like a candle. It consumes itself to light the way for others.

More than fifty million students were forced to stay home when schools across the country were shut down due to the coronavirus outbreak. Kitchens turned into classrooms and parents did their best to keep their kids learning. I've said many times that I'd be a teacher had I not pursued journalism, and I just loved a story I watched about how much out-of-work teachers missed their students. The video featured "teacher parades," cars filled with teachers honking and waving at their students, who lined neighborhood streets. Adorable kids waved and held up handmade signs that read, "We miss you!" Other stories highlighted how countless teachers reached out to their students online, one physical education instructor doing jumping jacks in his house as his students did the same in theirs. Using every technological format, educators did their best to engage with their pupils and keep up with lesson plans. I'm not surprised by the creativity and dedication of teachers, but I think every parent out there—including me—loves and respects our teachers even more than we already did.

A heart without dreams is like a bird without feathers.

—SUZY KASSEM

Anything making your heart flutter today?

> Out of difficulties grow miracles. —*Jean de La Bruyère*

Savannah joked that it was dust in her living room that caused her to tear up when we aired video of a mom finally meeting her miracle baby during the COVID-19 crisis. You couldn't help getting choked up watching the new mom cradle her baby for the first time twelve days after she gave birth to little Walter. Because she was battling the coronavirus, doctors at a Bay Shore, New York, hospital had to put Yanira Soriano in a medically induced coma, during which time she gave birth. Yanira breathed with the help of a ventilator for eleven days. Dr. Benjamin Schwartz told *Today*, "We didn't know if this little boy would ever meet his mom. She was in critical condition." Dr. Schwartz said his patient's three other children were extremely relieved to see their mom wheeled out of the hospital, as were the grateful health care workers whom Yanira acknowledged from behind her mask. "It was this powerful, human moment," said Dr. Schwartz. "We needed this so badly. We need something to celebrate." Oh my, yes. Welcome, Walter!

> Grief is the price we pay for love.
>
> —*Dr. Colin Murray Parkes*

When *Today* launched a "Miscarriage Matters" series, the goal was to offer the raw and poignant testimony of women who'd lost a baby. Some talked of shame, others isolation. Included was our own Kate Snow along with Dylan, who shared her perspective following tremendous grief: "If there's one thing I've realized during my short time as a mom, we have very little control over what happens." Other moms discussed the anguish of getting pregnant following a miscarriage, rife with what-ifs and a deep fear of growing attached. We could all use some input on what to say and not say to friends or family who've lost their child. At this second, many moms or almost moms are struggling and scared and suffering. I think the move toward less silence and more support is promising. With statistics indicating one in four pregnancies results in miscarriage, plenty of women, men, and families need both comfort and a voice.

Sometimes you have to get knocked down lower than you have ever been, to stand up taller than you ever were.

We can grow through what we go through!

An arch consists of two weaknesses, which, leaning one against the other, make a strength.

Did you just picture a rainbow? I did.

PS: Happy birthday, Hala!

We fall. We break. We fail. But then . . . We rise. We heal.
We overcome. We rise. We heal. We overcome.

I posted this the morning *Today* aired a video tribute to the strength
of the human spirit in the face of the spreading coronavirus. In two
minutes and fifty-seven seconds, all of the facts and figures became
faces—of hospital workers, first responders, scientists, and the se-
questered. The song "Rise Up" by Andra Day played in the background. "You will rise up, rise up . . ." You couldn't watch it without
crying and feeling immense gratitude for the brave helpers working
endless hours, risking their lives yet still finding the strength to dance
together and laugh. Moving, too, were images of the quarantined,
doing their best to take care of each other, often using music to beat
back feelings of isolation and fear. Handmade signs safely shared
their heartfelt messages: "Thank you, truck drivers," "Thanks for
the groceries," "Thank you all in emergency for saving my wife's
life," "Happy Birthday Papa Joe." My goodness. I think we all needed
a good cry, and this moving video unleashed our tears. We rise. We
heal. We overcome.

You can do anything, but not everything.

I'm not great at saying it, but I think the word "no" is the key to this one.

> Breath is the power behind all things. I breathe in and know that good things will happen.
>
> —*Tao Porchon-Lynch*

Well, then, let's try it! Big breath in . . . huuuuuuuuu. Slowly release it . . . wooooooooo. Repeat.

(Good things are coming!)

The best way to predict the future is to create it.

—PETER DRUCKER

That puts our hands on the wheel! With enough drive, *we* create the road map of our life.

HK

> So powerful is the light of unity that it can illuminate the
> whole world. —*Bahá'u'lláh*

Unity can illuminate just one neighborhood, too. I love James Corden—such a funny and kind soul, like the male version of Ellen. I'm not surprised James is the product of sweet parents, whom he interviewed from his garage during the COVID-19 crisis. Chatting via the internet, his parents, Malcolm and Margaret, were sitting in the UK home where James grew up. During their conversation, James rolled video of his father playing the saxophone and clarinet in the family's driveway as neighbors gathered around and swayed to the music, socially separated. The Cordens were so cute; Margaret even took requests! Malcolm explained that he initially held a solo concert because the local vicar suggested he play "Amazing Grace" to unify the neighborhood. It was such a hit that he committed to a performance every Thursday evening, the time when Britons participate in Clap for Our Carers, a way to applaud health care workers. I love the double-duty unity here, bringing together both a neighborhood and a country. Well done, Cordens.

Our greatest weakness lies in giving up. The most certain way to succeed is always to try just one more time.

—*Thomas A. Edison*

Is there anything you can try one more time today? I may take another shot at cleaning out my closet . . .

I don't know who needs to hear this right now, but if you're going through a rough time . . . don't cut your bangs.

Ouch! It never works out and takes *so* long to correct such a tempting—but rookie—mistake. This was actually a *thing* during the coronavirus crisis. With barbershops and salons closed, people resorted to managing their own hair trims, cuts, and color. The internet blew up with photos of bad haircuts at the hands of well-intentioned family members and friends. When Joel asked me to buzz his hair, I was terrified, having never used electric clippers. Because he and I were doing a "digital detox," I couldn't even watch a how-to video on YouTube! On the back porch, we started on the clipper's 3 setting, but Joel kept asking me to clip it closer. "I can't!" I declared, shaking. Haley was outside with us holding a paintbrush, and as the hair kept dropping, she tried to paint Daddy's hair back on! In the end, Joel was relieved to have his hair cut, and I was just glad I didn't draw blood. Honey, it just proves that no matter who cuts your hair, you always look great!

I am not lazy; I am on energy saving mode.

Yes! We need to save juice so we have energy for the long haul. Recharge today?

We met for a reason. Either you're a blessing or a lesson.

What a positive way to look at all of our relationships, past and present. Blessings we embrace; lessons we learn from.

> Asking for help does not mean that we are weak or incompetent. It usually indicates an advanced level of honesty and intelligence.   —*Anne Wilson Schaef*

When the 2020 Summer Olympics were delayed a year due to the pandemic, I spoke with superstar athlete Michael Phelps about his thoughts regarding what the postponement means for competitors. "It's tough," he said. "We know exactly when it's going to come and our bodies are ready for it and then we have to wait." Michael encouraged athletes to try to view the delay as an opportunity to fine-tune their skills. In recent years, the swimming legend has shared his own struggle with depression, so he understood how important it was for anxiety-ridden athletes to protect their mental health. "If you are in a spot where you need help, to reach out and ask for help. It was something that was very difficult for me to do, but it changed my life," he said, adding, "To be honest, it saved my life." Michael says he continues to work with a therapist, which allows him to be himself—a husband and father of three. What an important message for his fellow Olympians—and for us all—during any difficult time in our lives.

> Faith is unseen but felt, faith is strength when we feel we have none, faith is hope when all seems lost.
>
> —*Catherine Pulsifer*

A mother and daughter from New Orleans relied on faith to endure an epic battle with COVID-19. I met them on the other side of their challenge, all smiles and praise for God's grace. Nursing assistant Bridgette Robinson found herself in need of medical care, spending weeks on a ventilator fighting off the virus. Her daughter, Sylvia, worked as a nurse in the very hospital where her mom was struggling to survive. "It was definitely scary and heartbreaking," Sylvia said. "Especially the fact that she's my best friend." When I interviewed the pair on *Today*, Bridgette recalled hearing her grandson's voice on the phone when she woke up. "All I could think about is my grandson, and he was like, 'Grandma, I need you, I love you, I need you, Grandma.' I was just thinking . . . *I gotta get back to him.*" As a surprise, I asked Blake Shelton to join us live and sing his song "God Gave Me You." Before he did, Blake acknowledged the women's beautiful relationship. "You've got each other, and that's what this is really all about. Literally a light shining bright on that screen right there."

Family: a little bit of crazy, a little bit of loud, and a whole lot of love.

I'm pretty sure this could have been a banner hanging in most homes during the COVID-19 crisis.

> Courage is fear holding on a minute longer.
>
> —*General George S. Patton*

As a survivor of breast cancer, I cannot imagine what it must be like for children to battle the disease, or to be a terrified parent watching their child endure treatments. As a "Morning Boost" on *Today*, we aired video of a surprise parade for a little girl named Mabel who had finished her final chemotherapy treatment for leukemia. Her parents had planned a big shindig for their "Mighty Mabel," but when the pandemic demanded social distancing, the party was canceled. But supportive friends and family rallied together and organized a pop-up parade, complete with a flashing fire truck and dozens of decorated cars, passengers waving signs through the windows. Words on one back windshield read: "NO MORE CHEMO!" The courageous three-year-old and her grateful parents were all smiles, as the celebration just kept rolling along.

Eat, drink, and be scary.

We had an all-out *Sesame Street*–themed Halloween in 2019. T-shirts represented all of our cast favorites.

My mom: Cookie Monster
Hope: a cookie
Haley: Abby
Joel: Big Bird
Me: Elmo
Hala: Grover in Dubai

Friends joined in as Rosita, Zoe, Ernie, and Bert. We walked in a colorful pack singing "Sunny Day," which I'm sure was quite annoying to some fellow trick-or-treaters, but we just kept repeating it. Haley loved it, and Hope experienced her first Halloween in New York City, where collecting candy means stopping into mom-and-pop shops or accepting treats from neighbors sitting out on their stoops. It's such a fun experience that I'm already looking forward to next year. (We'll see if *Sesame Street* takes a backseat to a new favorite!)

I don't have anything to wear. I'm also out of hangers.

Whether at home or work, every one of my closets is jam-packed. I know it, Joel knows it, and my coworkers know it. Viewers got a glimpse of the overflow, too, thanks to a segment featured in the *Hoda & Jenna* hour. During the pandemic, Jenna was working from home and I was working out of my dressing room for the several-minute chat we called "Unscripted," when we talked about random topics. I'm not proud of this, but my dressing room is utter chaos, clothes hanging haphazardly and outfits bursting forth from the closets. Honestly, I simply don't notice it, but apparently, one viewer couldn't unsee it during the several weeks of "Unscripted." The same guy kept tweeting me over and over, "Close your closet door!" All I could do was laugh. My apologies, sir.

> There is no bad time for good news. —*Stephen King*

I love actor John Krasinski, and I *really* love an idea he executed beautifully with his gift of being both hilarious and sincere. In the midst of the devastating coronavirus crisis, he started an online "network" called SGN—"Some Good News." John broadcast from his home office, complete with an SGN sign hand-drawn by his daughters. One day, John featured a live chat with a fifteen-year-old cancer patient named Coco whose return home after her final chemotherapy treatment went viral in a heartwarming video shot from inside her car. John asked Coco what it was like to see her waving, cheering neighbors lining the street—safely separated—to welcome her home. "I was so surprised," she said. "We turned the corner and I saw our friends, then I saw more friends, then my family!" Coco went on to kindly thank her doctors, nurses, and everyone staying home to protect people like her with compromised immune systems. What a gracious kid. Thanks for the positive news, John, and be well, Coco!

Life is way too short to be a grump.

This quote sure seems to be the way Annette Muller lives her life. *Today* covered the story of eighty-two-year-old Annette and her daughter Kelly, who routinely checked on her quarantined mom during the COVID-19 crisis. One day, Kelly was greeted in the window by her grinning mother holding an empty bottle in one hand and a sign in the other that read: "Need More Wine." Ha! Kelly said her mom has always maintained a sense of humor despite a series of hardships, including the devastating loss of her husband and daughter to cancer and the last three years watching a son's battle with the disease. Through it all, Annette keeps smiling. Taking turns, Kelly and her siblings checked on their mom each day and chatted with her through the window. "She means the world to us," Kelly said, "and yes, in case anyone is wondering, I did get her wine!" Cheers, Annette, to you, your family, and your positive outlook on life!

> Life is found in the glass of spilled milk and in the long, narrow hallway filled with socks and soccer balls.
>
> —*Joanna Gaines*

I just feel good whenever Joanna Gaines is around. Talking with her is like sipping on hot chocolate; the room just feels cozier. When she released her cookbook *Magnolia Table, Volume 2: A Collection of Recipes for Gathering*, she shared several of her favorite comfort-food recipes on *Today*, including one for cookies named after one of her adorable kids. In the cookbook she writes, "Our son Crew tagged along for the final recipe tasting for this book, and when these cookies hit the table, he had more than his fair share." I just thought it might be nice today for your kitchen to smell like cinnamon and vanilla. If you search for "Crew's Cookies" on the *Today* website, you'll find the recipe. Or pick up a copy of Joanna's beautiful cookbook for yourself or for someone who could use a cup and a half of cozy.

> If I know what love is, it is because of you.
>
> —*Hermann Hesse*

It's a long story, but I'm an ordained minister. I'd never have imagined that would come in handy during the pandemic, but it did. I was honored to officiate a couple's wedding, virtually, as countless other couples had to cancel their big day. As a surprise for his disappointed fiancée, John Sizer coordinated with *Today* to hold an online wedding. John organized a fake Zoom call, pretending friends wanted to toast what would have been his and Melanie Mulvill's wedding weekend. When their pastor popped onto the call, Melanie was confused. My face further left her stymied. But once Melanie realized what was happening, she was all in! After some brief vows, I pronounced them husband and wife. (Their pastor later sealed the deal.) One last surprise was country singer Russell Dickerson's joining the call to sing their first-dance song, "Yours." What a sweet couple, and a very moving experience for everyone. Even Joel, sitting next to me off camera, shed some tears. Congratulations, Sizers, and yes, Savannah . . . I will renew your vows with Mike.

Sleep doesn't help
if it's your soul
that's tired.

I think that's the difference between the words "tired" and "weary."

HK

Being a nurse is to give your hands to serve and your heart to love.

A group of nurses at Vanderbilt University Medical Center in Nashville joined each other on the roof of the hospital during the coronavirus pandemic. Angela Gleaves, one of the five nurses, posted a photo on Facebook showing her and her coworkers gathered on the helipad. She wrote: "We prayed over the staff in our unit as well as all of the hospital employees." Angela added that prayers were also said for patients, their families, and colleagues around the world. At a time when many hospitals weren't allowing families to visit, thank goodness for the selfless, loving nurses, doctors, and other hospital workers who cared for our loved ones in such an unsettling environment. Angela—a registered nurse for twenty-two years—told *Today*, "It was a great moment. There was a little bit of wind, and I felt like it was God pushing us to care for these patients and do what we're trained to do." Thank you, Angela, and your fellow nurses Sarah, Beth, Tanya, and McKenzie. We were praying for you and all of the angels like you, too.

If you're always racing to the next moment, what happens to the one you're in?

Good for you for taking this very moment for yourself!

The heart will break, but broken live on.   —*Lord Byron*

I used to live and work in Fort Myers, Florida, so a video clip we aired on *Today* was extra special to me. In a show of support during the pandemic, police officers in Fort Myers configured more than a dozen cruisers—lights flashing—in the shape of a giant heart in front of Lee Memorial Hospital. Officers stood beside their vehicles in the parking lot, some making the shape of a heart with their hands. Signs in the center of the heart read: "FMPO THANKS YOU." Officers deliberately created the heart during a shift change so a large number of hospital workers could easily see how much the city loved and appreciated them. Fort Myers—the City of Palms and big hearts.

With God, all things are possible.   —*Matthew 19:26*

Whether you're listening to Dolly Parton sing or talk, she just feels like a ray of sunshine. Dolly was even wearing a sunny yellow shirt the day I asked her to share her favorite quote with me on *Today*. She chose the above segment of a Bible verse, explaining that it has guided and comforted her throughout her life, even more so during the global pandemic. "God is able to clear everything up. God is able to heal," she said. "God is able to open people's eyes, open people's hearts. He's able to do anything *if* we allow it." She added that without faith, we "drift along like leaves in the wind." She said that looking within ourselves to a higher wisdom helps combat fear of the unknown, during a pandemic or any challenge that comes our way in life. "It's natural to be afraid, but you cannot let fear be the ruler. . . . You kind of got to work through on that and just ask God to strengthen you." Beautiful insights, Dolly. We can't get enough of your warmth and wisdom!

> The best way to find yourself is to lose yourself in the service of others.
>
> —*Mahatma Gandhi*

Have you seen the amazing video featuring the surprise reunion of a mother and son in Texas? Don't miss the beautiful moment! At her police swearing-in ceremony, Erika Benning is seen waiting for her husband to pin on her badge. Then, in walks her son Giovanni, a sergeant in the US Army. She hasn't seen him in two years! In shock, her hands fly to her mouth and she breaks down, head bowed. Giovanni wraps his arms around her, and then Dad hugs them both. "I've wanted to be a police officer since I was four years old," Erika said. "And then to have my son pin my badge. It was overwhelming." We aired the video as a "Morning Boost" but could have renamed it "Morning Boohoo." I was so choked up that my coanchor Craig had to finish reading the script. As a mom and an American, I can't adequately express my gratitude and admiration for the Bennings' service and sacrifice. We love you! Maybe hug someone you love today, someone you're lucky enough to have by your side.

You can't cross the sea
by merely standing
and staring at the water.

—RABINDRANATH TAGORE

Hmm. Is this the day you finally set sail?

If opportunity doesn't knock, build a door.

—*Milton Berle*

I like this because it's proactive. Instead of wishing or waiting for something, we're encouraged to give opportunity a place to walk through. I consider the "door" our being prepared—being our best selves—so not only do we attract opportunities, we're ready for them when they come a-knockin'.

> The connections we make in the course of a life—maybe
> that's what heaven is.   —*Fred Rogers*

Prior to the release of the movie *A Beautiful Day in the Neighborhood*, I interviewed the cast. Tom Hanks played the gentle Fred Rogers. "The requirement to slow down," he said, "was one of the first true physical attributes I had to adopt." In the movie, we learn that Fred often didn't edit out the flubs he made while taping *Mister Rogers' Neighborhood* because he wanted kids to know we all make mistakes. Love that! I love even more what Fred said as he accepted a Lifetime Achievement Emmy award: "All of us have special ones who have loved us into being. Would you just take, along with me, ten seconds to think of the people who have helped you become who you are?" What an easy, loving idea. Ten seconds . . . maybe right now?

> If you let yourself be overcome by sorrow, you will drown in it. —*Solomon Northup, from* 12 Years a Slave

Today may just be the perfect day to reach out to someone who's treading water.

Go the extra mile. It's never crowded.

Speaking of going the extra mile, my NBC colleague did just that following her coverage of the COVID-19 crisis. Correspondent Janis Mackey Frayer spent five weeks traveling through Wuhan, China; Japan; and the UK covering the pandemic, then self-quarantined for fourteen days. In that span of time, Janis was away from her husband and young son for forty-nine days. Finally, she could rejoin her family! Her husband taped the mother-son reunion, her little one jumping up and down as Janis made a beeline for him. *So* beautiful! Both wearing masks, the two grabbed each other and held tight, basking in the long-awaited hug. On her Twitter feed, Janis posted the video and her thoughts on their days apart. "Yes, every one of them was hard—the worry, the decisions, the failed plans, isolation. Our little guy has been brave and resilient . . . and this was easily the best. hug. ever." Thank you, Janis, for your important work, and for doing the right thing to protect us all as your heart was breaking.

> To be fully seen by somebody, then, and be loved anyhow—
> this is a human offering that can border on miraculous.
>
> —*Elizabeth Gilbert*

There's a resort in Mexico that Joel and I consider "our place." We'll probably never bring the kids there because we want it to be *our* romantic, relaxing getaway. In November 2019, we'd escaped there and were enjoying our usual indulgences: beach time, tequila toasts, massages. One night, we were so relaxed post-massage that I suggested we skip dinner and hit the hay. Instead, Joel convinced me to grab a quick bite. We wandered out to a table that he'd asked the hotel to set out in the sand. Nothing seemed out of place; we'd done that before. After a delicious meal, Joel started giving a sweet speech to me, as he sometimes does. Then he got down on one knee and proposed. Both of us were in tears. The ring design? All him, which truly touched me. The evening was perfect! Everything unfolded so naturally, like the tropical breeze and the lapping waves at our favorite place. I didn't think I could feel any closer to Joel, but . . . I do.

Any change, even a change
for the better, is always
accompanied by drawbacks
and discomforts.

—Arnold Bennett

This is so important to remember so we don't quit. What feels like a mistake—*Why did I do this??*—may just be Change saying, "I'm making you work so hard because you'll be *really* proud of yourself at the end of this."

HK

> When you arise in the morning, think of what a precious privilege it is to be alive; to breathe, to think, to enjoy, to love.
> —*Marcus Aurelius*

I fell in love with US figure skater Adam Rippon—as did countless others—during the 2018 Winter Olympics in Pyeongchang, South Korea. Not only was he inspiring, making his Olympic debut at twenty-eight, Adam's positive energy was simply contagious. When he joined Savannah and me on set, it was as if a hand grenade of humor and joy exploded in the room. It didn't matter whether Adam was losing or winning his competitions; he was always smiling. One day on-air with him, I marveled at his relentless determination to have fun.

Me: Who's having a better time at the Olympics than Adam Rippon?

Adam: Maybe someone who has actually won them? [Huge smile on his face.]

Ha! Adam *did* win—a bronze medal in the team competition. Keep inspiring us, Adam!

> Do what you can, with what you have, where you are.
> —*Theodore Roosevelt*

When people were restricted by distancing and quarantines during the coronavirus crisis, I loved seeing all the creative ways we worked around the isolation. One of my favorites was crafted by the Torchia family, who turned their garage into a nightclub so Jack Torchia had a place to celebrate his twenty-first birthday. As a surprise, Jack's mom, dad, and sister led Jack to the garage, complete with a sign that read, "Must be 21 or older to enter." Jack's dad served as the bouncer, asking for ID and checking it with a flashlight. Inside the "club," music was pumping and Jack's mom served as bartender. "Welcome to Club Quarantine! What brings you in tonight?" When Jack replied, "My twenty-first birthday," shot glasses came out and the bartender declared there would be free shots for Jack, the bouncer, the server (his sister), and herself. How sweet that they went to so much trouble to celebrate a special birthday for Jack. Cheers to the Torchias and to everyone who refused to let a pandemic steal their milestones.

Sadness is but a wall between two gardens.

—*Kahlil Gibran*

What a beautiful image. Beauty awaits us on either side of pain.

Nobody can do for little children what grandparents can do. Grandparents sort of sprinkle stardust over the lives of little children.

—*Alex Haley*

When we were enduring the coronavirus crisis, everyone soaked up the sweet videos of drive-by birthday celebrations to keep our grandparents safe. One video showed a grandma waiting in her driveway, unsure of what surprise was headed her way. Then, around the corner rolled a car filled with her daughter and grandkids holding signs and singing, balloons blowing in the wind and one grandson popping up through the moonroof wearing an ear-to-ear smile. She was overjoyed, circling her arms in what she called a "virtual hug." Boy, did you weep a lot during those trying times? I sure did.

PS: Happy birthday, Adel!

> Gratitude will shift you to a higher frequency and you will attract much better things.
>
> —*Rhonda Byrne*

I'm not someone who talks about my sex life with anyone. There's nothing wrong with doing that; it's just not my thing. While many of us are private about the topic, we're apparently happy to learn more, and that's why renowned sex therapist Dr. Ruth Westheimer was wildly popular on radio, television, and as a bestselling author. When she appeared on *Today* to talk about *Ask Dr. Ruth*, a documentary about her life, the vibrant ninety-one-year-old shared that while her Jewish parents died during the Holocaust, she survived, sent by her mother to an orphanage in Switzerland. Ruth later trained in Jerusalem as a sniper in a paramilitary organization and was seriously wounded in action during Israel's War of Independence. While I admire the doctor's ability to educate us about sex, I loved listening to her talk about how grateful she is to be alive. "From my background, all the things I've survived," she said, "I have an obligation to live large and make a dent in this world." And you have, Dr. Ruth!

November 24

Forget your troubles and dance.   —*Bob Marley*

Sadly, milestone events of all kinds were canceled when the pandemic struck, including senior proms. On *Today*, Al gave one high school class the surprise of a lifetime when he threw them a virtual prom! First, he sent seniors at Douglas County West in Nebraska a sign featuring his face and "Prom?" as well as boxed corsages and boutonnieres. Next, Al not only led the kids in a dance party, he announced the prom king and queen, crowned by their parents. There was even a surprise pop-in by singer Demi Lovato because one student considered the superstar her singing idol. The deserving senior class and their families had endured severe flooding the year before, followed this year by a pandemic. The kids did their part during both disasters, this time cleaning medical supplies and delivering food to seniors. They truly earned such a special treat. When the virtual prom ended, there was Al wearing that huge Roker smile and offering his best wishes: "Class of 2020, congratulations!"

> But every house where Love abides and Friendship is a guest, is surely home, and home, sweet home, for there the heart can rest.
>
> —*Henry Van Dyke*

Right around Thanksgiving 2019, singer Idina Menzel performed her song "At This Table" on *Today*. As I sat in the studio listening to the beautiful music and lyrics, I immediately thought of Maria Shriver. I'd just had a conversation with her about how, throughout her life, she's always invited people into her home for a meal. Hosting people, breaking bread, and creating a comfortable setting where everyone can let their guard down has always been meaningful to her. As Idina sang, I downloaded "At This Table" and texted it to Maria. After the show, the two of us listened to it together in the makeup room. I gotta say . . . we had a moment. Maria, who rarely tears up, got misty-eyed as phrases like "everybody matters" and "come as you are" floated through the air. Always one to deflect compliments, Maria didn't say much. The next day she pulled me aside and told me how much it mattered to her that I sent the song. Funny how just hitting "send" sometimes touches someone.

> What we carry defines who we are. —*Mitch Albom*

I love all of Mitch Albom's books, but my favorite is *Finding Chika*. Mitch shares the story of how he and his wife, Janine, battled for two years to save their five-year-old adopted daughter, Chika, who developed a brain tumor. As her illness advanced, Mitch began carrying Chika around the house, from the couch to the bed or to wherever she needed to be. One day, as they were coloring at the kitchen table, Mitch told Chika he needed to go. When Chika asked him to stay and color, he said he had to work. She insisted they had to play. "But this is my job," he answered. Chika disagreed and told him, "Your job is carrying me." In the book, Mitch says that her words stuck with him, and that perhaps the biggest lesson Chika taught him is that what we carry defines who we are. Isn't that so beautiful? I was moved to tears. Said another way, whatever carries the full weight of our attention and devotion defines who we are as a person. Maybe think about what you're carrying?

There are two ways of spreading light: to be the candle or the mirror that reflects it. —*Edith Wharton*

In modern terms . . . tweeting something inspirational or retweeting it.

Every morning you have two choices:
continue to sleep with your dreams,
or wake up and chase them.

Grab some coffee and let the chase begin!

HK

> Everything will be okay in the end. If it's not okay, it's not the end.
>
> —*John Lennon*

This quote reminds me of a story my dear friend Jane shared with me while she was in the excruciating position of watching her father battle Parkinson's disease. I loved Jane's dad, Jim—one of the kindest souls I've ever known. One evening, Jane received a call from her dad's wife, asking if she would come over, saying that Jim was concerned he wouldn't make it through the night. As she drove the thirty minutes to their house, she racked her brain as to what to say that would soothe her dad. He'd always protected and comforted her, and now it was Jane's turn to ease his heart and mind. Walking down the hall to his bedroom, she still hadn't found the right words. But when she lay down next to her sweet, scared father, she simply took his hand and said, "Dad, I feel strongly that this is *not* how your story ends." They talked side by side until he fell asleep. As you might imagine, Jim's answering her phone call the next morning was everything.

Every child is a different kind of flower, and all together make this world a beautiful garden.

Oh, so beautiful . . . their little faces lifted toward the light, brightening the world with every color under the sun.

Exercise? I thought you said, "Extra fries."

Ha! I love all fries—thick cut, curly, truffle. But if I had to pick my "extra fries," I'd go curly with tons of Heinz ketchup.

Set your life on fire. Seek those who fan your flames.

—RUMI

When we allow people in who don't support us, we can get burned. Look for the fanners.

Missing someone is your heart's way of reminding you that you love them.

The COVID-19 pandemic tested the faith of people around the world. Not being able to gather together in church compounded the angst. I loved the creativity of a pastor who missed his flock at United Methodist Church in Huntsville, Texas. Someone posted a photo of what the pastor and his staff did: they printed photos of each congregant and attached them to the pews! Now when church members watched the livestreamed sermons they could "be together" in church. Amen to such a clever and heartfelt workaround.

> Hard work beats talent when talent doesn't work hard.
>
> —*Tim Notke*

I think I got used to rejection in my career field because I experienced so much of it early on. It took me twenty-seven interviews to land my first job in television broadcasting! I had the same experience playing high school basketball. We practiced, we lost, we practiced some more. I think if you're used to losing or being rejected, you'll make it, because hard work feels like a normal part of the process. People who bust their hump succeed because they never consider quitting; it's not an option. On the other hand, if someone's always been "the best" at something and then criticism comes their way, it may be so jarring—so unexpected—that they give up. Here's the message: People drop out, people! Don't quit, even when it's hard. Your slot's about to open up.

No one is useless in this world who lightens the burden of another.   —*Charles Dickens*

British poet Tom Roberts never dreamed he'd lighten the burden of so many people during the COVID-19 crisis. In his video "The Great Realisation," Tom set a poem he'd written to pictures and pretended to be a dad reading a bedtime story to his son. (If you missed it, it's worth a look.) Jenna and I—and twenty million other people—watched the video and were so moved by its hopeful message that we asked the twenty-six-year-old to join us from London. "We are consuming so much negativity, and rightly so because it's scary and there's so many people suffering," Tom said. "But at the same time, I really believe that people are incredibly resilient if you can give or suggest there might be even the smallest ray of hope." The message of the video is that one day we'll look back and see the good that came from something so bad. Humbled by the massive reaction, Tom said he was just doing his part; his family is all medical workers. And when he found out Jennifer Aniston had "liked" his video? "My head fell off," he said.

If you don't like where you are, move.
You are not a tree.

Sometimes it feels like we are, the deep roots of pain or fear making it seemingly impossible to move. The goal is to cut the roots and find our footing . . . so we can take that first step forward.

HK

> Believe you can and you're halfway there.
>
> —*Theodore Roosevelt*

I have a friend whose grandmother offered her similar advice: a job well planned is half done.

Mistakes are proof that you are trying.

So what if you fumble? At least you're in the game!

> The flower doesn't dream of the bee. It blossoms and the bee comes.
>
> —*Mark Nepo*

This is a call to action, right? The work we do on improving ourselves becomes a magnet for goodness.

> You can't experience simple joys when you're living life
> with your hair on fire.　　　　　　　　　　*—Emily Ley*

Well, then, NBC White House correspondent Kristen Welker must be *very* joyful. That woman's hair is never on fire! She's as cool as a cucumber and proved it beyond a doubt one day on the White House lawn. Kristen was reporting for MSNBC on a particularly windy afternoon, and strong gusts were thrashing her hair and coat collar as she spoke to Andrea Mitchell. Suddenly, a large stand light on her right crashed through her shot to the ground, causing Ms. Smooth to adjust a tiny bit. Immediately, the stand light on her left crashed across the screen. Boom! "It's a little windy out here, Andrea," was the only reference Kristen made to the near calamity, and she continued her report without missing a beat. We were all "blown away" by her composure and had a good laugh at a tweet by her hometown team, the Philadelphia Eagles, as the NFL draft kicked off.

Scouting report: Prospect clearly has superior knowledge of the game and raw talent to complement her speed. Elite ability to avoid contact in small spaces.

The first secret of success: believe in yourself.

—STEVE GOODIER

Yep—and it's not a secret. There it is . . . in writing.

HK

December 12

> Whoever loves much, performs much, and can accomplish much, and what is done in love, is done well.
>
> —*Vincent van Gogh*

In an effort to protect senior citizens, grocery stores around the country allowed the elderly to shop early during the COVID-19 crisis. Tyler Perry—ever generous—surprised shoppers in two Southern cities by paying for their groceries during the "high risk" hour. In forty-four Kroger locations in Atlanta, and twenty-nine Winn-Dixies in New Orleans, customers were overjoyed by his random act of kindness. I loved seeing the photos of shocked older folks in the checkout lines, some displaying their receipts, others teary-eyed. Having grown up impoverished, Tyler knows what it's like to feel afraid and vulnerable. Where there is need, there is Tyler. Around this time in 2018, he paid off nearly a half-million dollars in layaways for Christmas shoppers in Atlanta-area Walmarts. You truly embody this, Tyler: what is done in love, is done well.

> Just as despair can come to one only from other human beings, hope, too, can be given to one only by other human beings.
> —*Elie Wiesel*

My NBC colleague Stephanie Gosk covered a moving story of hope after a photo went viral during the COVID-19 crisis. When New York governor Andrew Cuomo made an urgent plea to medical workers from unaffected areas to relieve exhausted hospital staff in the city, tens of thousands of volunteers responded from all over the country, despite the risk of getting sick or even losing their lives. A dozen health care workers who flew in from Atlanta were captured in a beautiful photo taken during the flight. All smiles, everyone on board is holding their hands over their head, their fingers forming a heart. Love and support were winging their way toward our ravaged city. Bright spots popped up everywhere—free flights and hotel rooms were offered to the selfless volunteers. Medical students chose to graduate early to enter the fight; retired physicians rejoined the ranks to save lives. In the end, goodness won. During such a terrifying and painful time, we came to each other's rescue. Thank you.

It's not what's under the Christmas tree that matters but who's around it.

— *Charlie Brown, from* **A Charlie Brown Christmas**

M y family has the exact same "surprise" every Christmas. When Joel and I plan the holiday with my mom, Hala is allegedly staying in Dubai. Then there's that annual knock on the door.

Me: Well, who could that be?
Hala: Surprise!
My mom: Whaaat??? You're kidding me!

We capture the big moment on video, and I have to hand it to Hala. She sells it, giggling with glee as if it's the first time she's made a surprise visit. My mom's good, too, throwing her arms up in the air as if she hasn't seen Hala in ten Christmases. We do it every year and I love it. "Look, it's Hala!" (again).

Spilling coffee is the adult equivalent of losing your balloon.

Yes, and it's especially annoying after I've added the *perfect* amount of Coffee Mate.

No one has ever become poor by giving. —*Anne Frank*

There's so much about Christmastime—the dizzying mix of work, parties, family events, shopping, travel—that can put us in a holi*daze*. I suppose that's why a sermon Savannah described listening to at her church resonated with me. She said that her minister offered the congregation a plan for the holidays, a simple way to find meaning during a month filled with to-do lists and overindulgence. He outlined a two-week plan: Week one—consume less. Stop coveting so much food or stuff or news or whatever it is you're OD'ing on. Week two— give more. Give in ways you haven't before and do it often. Revolutionary? No, but it's super clear. I guess I just like her pastor's straightforward marching orders at such a hectic time of the year. Actually, it sounds like a solid plan throughout the year, too, doesn't it?

*Success isn't
permanent
and
failure isn't
fatal.*

—MIKE DITKA

I like the way this takes both ego and fear down a notch.

HK

> The littlest feet make the biggest footprints in our hearts.

Jenna shared a beautiful story on the air about what her daughter said after her grandfather George H. W. Bush passed away. She said that when the family awoke to the news on November 30, 2018, her husband, Henry, offered to take the kids so she could process the devastating loss. Jenna turned to Henry and said, "I can't believe this is happening right before Christmas." Her then-five-year-old daughter said to Henry, "Daddy, of course it's happening around Christmas. Gampy had to get up there with Ganny to decorate the Christmas tree." Oh, so heavenly! What a comforting image that little one tucked into Jenna's heart at such a sad time.

> There is no exercise better for the heart than reaching
> down and lifting people up.   —*John Holmes*

During the Christmas holidays, I watched a group of amazing people deck the halls for kids at the Memorial Sloan Kettering Cancer Center in New York. Guys on the center's Facilities Management Team worked through the night to surprise young patients with an amazing "holiday hallway" to wander through, complete with dazzling lights, Christmas villages, and churning trains. Because of carpenters, electricians, plumbers, and painters, a dark basement hallway was transformed into a festive extravaganza, a labor of love that's been under way for nearly thirty years. "It may have started out as a little bit of a competition between the shops," Jim Imparato said, "but it just took that one kid to come down and look at it, to see they're down, especially if they're coming back from a treatment. . . . It's a joy to see." On their own time, with their own dime, team members create the magical walkway each year. Watching the kids enjoy their surprise was an awesome gift I'll never forget. Way to go, Christmas Crew! You may look like tough guys, but clearly, you're all heart.

We can only be said to be alive in those moments when our
hearts are conscious of our treasures.

—*Thornton Wilder*

What a beautiful way to celebrate gratitude.

Four stages of life:

1. You believe in Santa Claus
2. You don't believe in Santa Claus
3. You are Santa Claus
4. You look like Santa Claus

I'm in stage three!

> Gratitude is the memory of the heart.
>
> —*Jean-Baptiste Massieu*

Craig Melvin has two young kids, so I know a story he covered about a Milwaukee father truly moved him. For seventeen years, Greg Phelps has suited up as Santa Claus and headed to his local hospital. "It always reminds me of the first time I saw Kyle as a two-and-a-half-pound baby in the NICU," he said. Just before Christmas, Greg's son Kyle was born three months early, and as a result, spent ninety-eight days in the neonatal intensive care unit. "A man came in dressed as Santa Claus and took pictures with all the babies," Greg recalled. "So for a few minutes, it helped to bring some hope and some joy." Several years after Kyle came home and the NICU Santa retired, Greg replaced him, knowing firsthand what the visits would mean to anxious families. Kyle, now twenty-one, joins his dad each year, his story of hope shared on a tag attached to the dozens of stuffed animals they hand out to families. Wow! Way to give back, Phelps family, again and again. Your gratitude sparkles like a Christmas tree.

> Optimism is a happiness magnet. If you stay positive, good things and good people will be drawn to you.
>
> —*Mary Lou Retton*

When I interviewed Yale psychology professor Laurie Santos about whether some people are wired to be happy more so than others, she said that while that may play a small role, there are steps each and every one of us can take to boost our mood. Laurie not only teaches an online course in happiness at Yale, she hosts a podcast called *The Happiness Lab*. To up our daily happiness quotient, she suggests taking slow, deep breaths, doing something kind for others, practicing gratitude, and getting enough rest and exercise. Following the story, my colleagues and I did a round robin of happiness tools on *Today*:

Savannah: yoga

Craig: corny jokes

Al: family

Me: Haley's giggle

Carson: a Bloody Mary

> A happy family is but an earlier heaven.
>
> —*George Bernard Shaw*

Growing up, my siblings and I were only allowed to open one gift on Christmas Eve. As you might imagine, technique was very important to ensure you chose the best night-before gift. We would take our time shaking, squeezing, and inspecting the shape of every gift under the tree. After we tore open "the one," it was so hard to sleep that night awaiting the big day when we could enjoy the rest of our presents. Our tradition now is for my sister, my mom, Joel, the kids, and me to head out to a small beach house and put up a big tree. We just hang out and cozy up to a fire, while Joel grills on the deck whether it's raining, snowing, or sleeting. I just love the magic of being together with nothing else to do but laugh, eat, and watch the little ones rekindle our holiday spirit. May you be where you want with people you love, as Christmas Eve unfolds in all its glory.

Christmas, my child, is love in action. Every time we love,
every time we give, it's Christmas.   —*Dale Evans*

I know it's probably a passing phase, but I loved watching Haley's adoration for her sister outweigh her desire for presents on Christmas morning in 2019. Not yet three years old, Haley was dressed in her red-and-white-striped pajamas wearing a Santa hat pulled down over her bedhead hair. She was cradling and staring at Hope's baby monitor, waiting for her little sister to wake up. Gifts under the tree, stockings bulging with presents—even Santa's leftover cookies were of no interest to her. "I love you, Hopey," Haley said into the small screen. Then, smack! She laid a big kiss on the side of the monitor. Next, she repeated what I'd said as best she could in that sweet little voice of hers: "Merry Christmas, Hope. We're coming to get you!" After staring at the screen for a bit more, she announced, "She movin', Mommy." Oh my goodness, my favorite present of all.

(Another gift during Christmastime was that Hope stood up all by herself!)

Feed your faith and your fears will starve to death.

Countless prayers were launched—and still are being launched—as we navigated the pandemic, desperate to starve both the virus and our deepest, darkest fears.

Now rest.
Tomorrow
be strong.

We always make sure to recharge our phones but sometimes forget to do the same with our bodies. Let's try to do better!

HK

Confidence is not "They will like me." Confidence instead is "I'll be fine if they don't."   —*Christina Grimmie*

We all want to be liked, but the truth is: you can't please 'em all, right?

Something beautiful is on the horizon. Keep on going.

What awaits *you* just beyond the sunrise or sunset? Surely it's a reward well worth what feels so challenging right now. Keep on keepin' on!

December 30

> Sometimes miracles are just good people with kind hearts.

Have you ever been moved to tears by the kindness of another person? I sure was following an interview I did with Drew Brees, one of the kindest people I know. The New Orleans Saints quarterback donated five million dollars to help feed people in Louisiana, which had been hit hard by the coronavirus. As I wrapped up our interview on *Today*, I told him that I felt his generosity would fuel others to donate, too. We exchanged "love you"s, and that's when the dam broke for me. I started bawling. You know when you simply can't reel in your emotions? That was me. My heart was breaking for my beloved New Orleans, for New York, our country, the world. And there was my friend Drew, giving and leading as he always does. Friday had arrived after a long week of COVID-19 coverage—a mind-bending mix of horrors and heroes—and I guess I just needed a good cry. Drew's message to New Orleans that morning was simple but meaningful, and it's a good one for us all, every day: hang in there and maintain hope.

> Take a leap of faith and begin this wondrous new year by believing. —*Sarah Ban Breathnach*

In 2019, Jenna gave me an idea for ringing in a new year. I was trying to figure out what to do with little kids for New Year's Eve, and I just fell in love with a tradition she's created for her family. Every New Year's Eve, they celebrate the last sunset of the year cuddled up with their kiddos. I love that! The glowing, setting sun is such a beautiful version of the ball dropping in Times Square. From now on, there will be paper hats and noisemakers and the pure joy of turning a borrowed tradition into an annual celebration of our own. We'll say goodbye to the sun and hello to a brand-new year . . . almost. Happy New Year's Eve!

Conclusion

....

Writing a conclusion right now is complicated. We face serious challenges in America, and the remedies—both medically and socially—remain undetermined. How ironic it is that 2020 has been a year where a vision for the future is anything but clear. I don't know about you, but I've never cried so much in a span of several months—tears of sadness, tears of joy, and often, tears of gratitude I wept with my cheek resting on my daughters' soft hair. I imagine you experienced the same whiplash of emotions, doing your best to navigate the surreal set of circumstances we found ourselves in during 2020. Our worlds were turned upside down—school and work came home, normalcy left the building, and there was nowhere to hide from an invisible foe. Immersed in hand sanitizer and uncertainty, we sent up prayers and laid down new rules at home, quickly breaking many in the name of family sanity. Events we relied on to mark milestones and make memories were stolen from us, graduation caps and team jerseys set aside. Still, when activities ceased, creativity soared, many of us tackling new hobbies and dusting off to-do lists. Sewing machines hummed across the land, churning out protective masks for family and neighbors. Companies shifted gears on a dime to produce lifesaving equipment for patients and frontline workers. Within weeks, when things got real, we figured out workarounds, sharing tips on covering up roots and trimming shaggy hair. We got a look-see into each other's living rooms as we Zoomed through happy hours and happy birthdays. Some of us spent our free time getting into shape, others rounded our curves, but *all* of us worried . . . about each other, empty cupboards, bills, derailed dreams. Then, an act of savagery further stressed our nation and protests erupted in the streets, demands for change sparking both intense discussion and destruction. Reform seemed to finally be within reach if it came in peace.

I began writing this book when life was still "normal." But several months in, both the virus and the urgent battle for change collided. The book then became a journal of sorts, documenting the best of us during the worst of times. In these pages, we have memorialized the way we cared for ourselves and each other as life felt out of control. Perhaps like you, I'm still processing what I've learned from these tumultuous times because they're not over. I do know I chose correctly in Joel, my measured, positive partner, who reassured me that everything would be okay. I know I'll never take hugging my mom or looking into someone's eyes without a computer screen or windowpane between us for granted. I've read a stack of books about the black experience in America and I'm open to learning more.

Right now it's June, and as I turn this book in to my publisher, I can only imagine the state of things as you read these words. How are you? Healthy and happy, I hope. I pray that you, our country, and the world are now on a bit more solid footing. I'm certain the grieving and the giving and the talking continue as we do our best to support one another, still stunned that our collective journey included a pandemic and nationwide protests. If in even some small way *This Just Speaks to Me* provided you comfort, I'm grateful. And because the road to healing includes helping, please consider sharing your copy with a friend or family member in need of a boost. I'll sign off now with a quote that might lift us up as we take a breath and tackle whatever's next with hope . . . and with each other.

Hope is the sun. It is light. It is passion.
It is the fundamental force for life's blossoming.
—DAISAKU IKEDA

Acknowledgments

First and foremost, I offer my utmost gratitude to you for connecting with me through this book. Whether we were together every day for a year, or in bursts of binge reading, I've loved every minute. We are better together in this life, aren't we—with all of the joy, surprise, sorrow, and love it bestows upon us. Thank you for being there.

Look at what your beautiful idea has done, Cait Hoyt. Book two. Thank you, my friend and CAA book agent, for realizing that quotes could be bundled, reflected upon, and shared. You always know what we need.

To the entire team at Penguin Random House—thank you for being *all in* on the next iteration of our original goal: to help people. Michelle Howry, executive editor—your unflappable can-do attitude is both comforting and contagious. To Ivan Held; Sally Kim; Alexis Welby and Katie Grinch; Ashley McClay and Emily Mlynek; Tiffany Estreicher, Katy Riegel, and Monica Cordova; Meredith Dros, Maija Baldauf, and Janice Kurzius; and Ashley Di Dio— huge and heartfelt thanks. How you manage to sustain so much collective and creative energy is astounding . . . and extremely appreciated. Your talents have elevated this book from the inside out and beyond. I know we've all felt grateful to work on such a positive, inspiring project during uniquely challenging times. Thank you, each and every one of you. You're amazing.

And finally, to the incomparable Jane Lorenzini, the best writer and dearest friend I have ever known. I still have a journal entry from twenty years ago about these words you wrote to me: "I'm all yours, you're all mine, and we are all ours." I treasure it . . . and you.